C0-AQI-901

BETTER SPEECH

AND

BETTER READING

A PRACTICE BOOK

By

LUCILLE D. SCHOOLFIELD

Co-author With JOSEPHINE B. TIMBERLAKE of
"Sounds the Letters Make"
and
"The Phonovisual Method"

Expression is but Revelation

EXPRESSION COMPANY

BOSTON   **MASSACHUSETTS**

COPYRIGHT, 1937, 1951, BY
LUCILLE D. SCHOOLFIELD

Copyright in the Philippine Islands

All rights reserved. Under the law the above
copyright protects the owner against copying
by any process whatsoever, for any purpose
whatsoever, any part of the contents of this
book.

Twenty-second printing, December 1972

To the Memory of

MY MOTHER

Lucy Dillard France Schoolfield

ACKNOWLEDGMENTS

The author wishes to express grateful appreciation to Miss Josephine B. Timberlake, Editor, *The Volta Review*, for her thoughtful criticism and generous encouragement in the revisions of the manuscript; and to her brother, J. Edwin Schoolfield, for his interest, cooperation and assistance in its preparation.

For permission to use the copyright material included in this volume, the compiler is indebted to the following authors and publishers, whose courtesy is gratefully acknowledged:

To *The American Boy* for "Jack O'Lantern," by Anna Chandler Ayer; "A Hint to the Wise," by Pringle Barret; and "Fireflies," by Helen Virginia Frey.

To the *American Junior Red Cross News* for "Lazy Time," by Jean Gray Allen; and "Lessons in Unnatural History," by Eliot Kays Stone.

To A. A. Beauchamp for "The Lollypops," from *Sunny Days*, by Cordia Thomas.

To the *Board of Christian Education of the Presbyterian Church* for "Thanksgiving," from *Verses for Children*, by Cecil Trout Blancké.

To the *Child Training Association* and *The Junior Home Magazine* for "The Zebra at the Zoo," and "About a Very Cross Lion Named John," by Gertrude duBois; "If I Had a Pony," by Gorton V. Carruth; and "Nature's Wash Day," by Marguerite Gode.

To *The Christian Science Monitor* for "Which?" by Joyce L. Brisley.

To *Country Life* for "Bird Language," by Florence B. Steiner.

To Merle Crowell for his poem "If I Were an Elephant."

To Sarah J. Day for her poem "The Crocus," from *Mayflowers to Mistletoe*.

To *Dodd, Mead and Company* for "A Bunch of Roses," by John Bannister Tabb.

To E. P. Dutton & Company for "The Lonely Goldfish," by Alicia Aspinwall.

To Walter Prichard Eaton for "The Birches," from *Echoes and Realities*.

To Eldridge Entertainment House for "Lost," by Alfred I. Tooke, from *Recitation Stunts for Little Folks*.

To Aileen Fisher for her poems, "Company," "Desserts," "Drawing," "Fall," "Goldfish," "Hiding," "The Moon," "The Package"; and "April Music" and "Ladybug," from her book *The Coffee Pot Face*.

To Mrs. Laura Stedman Gould and Mrs. K. A. McCartney for "The Dearest Land," by Edmund Stedman.

To *The Instructor* for "September," by Solveig Paulson; "Yours and Mine" and "Valentine," by Frances Gorman Risser. Used by permission of F. A. Owen Publishing Company.

To *John Lane The Bodley Head Limited* for "The Wonderful World," by W. B. Rands.

To the *Journal of Education* for "Christmas Bells," by Frances Kirkland.

To Mrs. Aline Kilmer for "Easter," by Joyce Kilmer.

To Richard Kirk for his poems "Cock-a-Doodle Doo" and "Our Two Gardens."

To *J. B. Lippincott Company* for the two poems: "Our Flag," and "Biddy Hen and Yellow Duck," from *Citizenship Readers* by E. Ringer and L. Downie.

To Robert M. McBride & Company for "April Music" and "Ladybug," by Aileen Fisher.

To *Rand McNally & Company* and *Child Life* for "Little Charlie Chipmunk," by Helen Cowles LeCron; "My Airedale Dog," by W. L. Mason, used by special permission of Mrs. W. L. Mason; "A Humming Bee," and "Twink! Twink!" by Wilhemina Seegmiller, used by permission of her sister, Margaret Seegmiller.

To the *Macmillan Company* for "Winter" and "The Clouds," by Christina G. Rossetti; and "Kittens," from the *Gates-Huber Work-Play Books*.

To *Marshall Hughes Company* for "When I Go Fishing."

To *Methuen & Company, Ltd.* for "A Chinese Nursery Rhyme," translated by I. T. Headland.

To *Milton Bradley Company* for "The Clock," from *The Kindergarten Review*.

To *Oxford University Press* for "Fairy Umbrellas," by Lucy Diamond.

To *F. A. Owen Publishing Company*, Dansville, N. Y. for "Where the Fairies Dwell," by Nina Willis Walter, from "Primary Plans and Projects."

To G. P. Putnam's Sons for "Whistles," "Brooms," and "The Goldfish," by Dorothy Aldis.

To *St. Nicholas* for "Swinging," by Marion E. Thorpe Diller; "Starry Nights" and "Whistle," by Leonard Twynham.

To the *Saturday Review of Literature* for "Cock-a-Doodle Doo," by Richard Kirk.

To *Charles Scribner's Sons* for "Fire in the Window," by Mary Mapes Dodge; "Happy Thought," "The Lamplighter," and "Rain," by Robert Louis Stevenson.

To *J. H. Shultz* for "A Message," by Maud N. Goetting, and "The Sky is a Blue, Blue Sea," by Mrs. Isla Paschal Richardson, from *The Kindergarten-Primary Magazine*.

To *The Volta Review* for "The Best Tree," "Budding Trees," "Can You?" "March," "New Year Prayer," by Mildred Evans; and "October," by J. Evelyn Willoughby.

To *Frederick Warne & Company, Ltd.* for "Little Wind" and "Under the Window," by Kate Greenaway.

To the *Yale University Press* for "Days," from *Blue Smoke*, by Karle Wilson Baker.

Personal permission has been received from the following authors for the use of their poems which appear in this volume, for which the compiler expresses her sincere appreciation: Dorothy Aldis, Jean Gray Allen, Alicia Aspinwall, Cecil Trout Blancké, Gorton V. Carruth, Merle Crowell, Marion E. Thorpe Diller, Gertrude duBois, Walter Prichard Eaton, Mildred Evans, Aileen Fisher, Marguerite Gode, Richard W. Kirk, Helen LeCron, Francis Gorman Risser, Eliot Kays Stone, Alfred I. Tooke, and Leonard Twynham.

FOREWORD

This book was originally designed to be used only in speech classes for the correction of articulatory defects, but teachers in other fields, on seeing the manuscript, expressed the belief that it would meet the needs of a much wider area. At their suggestion, the title was changed from *Better Speech* to *Better Speech and Better Reading*.

Their comments follow:

A regular classroom teacher: "This is a book that can be used not only for speech work in the classroom, but also to teach children who have difficulty with reading."

A teacher of remedial reading: "It is a book that can be placed in the hands of the children. The carefully classified word lists and practice sentences give opportunity to clarify visually vowels and consonants so often confused by children who have reading disabilities."

A teacher of young students of lip reading: "Our group will welcome the chance of integrating the practice words of the lip reading class with the practice words of the speech class and the vocabulary of the primary grades."

A teacher of the deaf: "These carefully selected words and sentences from the primary child's own vocabulary provide in attractive form the necessary practice formerly obtainable only on dull and tiresome drill charts."

In these days, when the voice becomes the personality of the speaker through the radio; when reading difficulties are being analyzed and classified by scientists; when lip reading classes spring up like mushrooms in public schools; when the deaf are no longer allowed to remain speechless; when attention is focused on perfect enunciation in an increasing number of activities, it is hoped that this volume of practice exercises will prove of benefit.

Certainly, when every individual uses his organs of speech properly, the difficulties which beset the hard-of-hearing and the deaf, as well as those with normal hearing, will be considerably lessened. The author offers this volume—a practice book for *Better Speech and Better Reading*—as a step toward the goal of *Perfect Enunciation for Every Pupil*.

TABLE OF CONTENTS

---

* Consonants and vowels are classified according to the Merriam-Webster New International Dictionary—(1935); consonants, according to the *place* of formation, as the lip, lip-teeth, etc.; vowels, according to the *tongue-position*, as front, central, etc. International Phonetic Alphabet symbols are those given in the Merriam-Webster.

Table of Contents

Table of Contents

Articulation Test Material

Poems

Indexes

PLAN OF THE BOOK

Better Speech and Better Reading was designed by a teacher of speech correction to aid in the correction of articulatory defects by providing practice material *within the comprehension of the elementary pupil.*

The text of the book is devoid of theoretical discussion. It makes no attempt to discuss the techniques of correcting speech defects, but provides practice material for the use of the speech correction pupil, *after* he has been taught to produce the sound correctly, yet needs practice in making the correct pronunciation habitual.

There are many books on the market today which contain very helpful speech exercises. Frequently, however, their scope is limited in content or grade, and the need for appropriate practice material for elementary pupils often requires a search through many volumes. This book attempts to meet this need by providing in one volume a variety of exercises so flexible that they may be easily adapted to different grade levels, and sufficiently comprehensive to meet everyday demands.

The word lists are based on *A Reading Vocabulary for the Primary Grades* (Revised 1935) by Arthur I. Gates, and *The Teacher's Word Book* by Edward L. Thorndike. Effort was made to choose both test and drill words from the lists for the primary grades. In the more difficult consonant blends, this was manifestly impossible. All words, therefore, not found in the Gates List or the first 1500 words of the Thorndike List are indicated by asterisks.

As recommended by the *National Society for the Prevention of Blindness*, a large type is used.

Better Speech and Better Reading offers in one volume:

I. Practice Material, which Provides for Individual Differences.

Each consonant and vowel has its own practice material. The teacher has only to turn to the designated sound to find organized drills for practice.

Word lists are graded in difficulty. All drill words not in the Gates or Thorndike Primary Word lists are indicated by asterisks. Thus the teacher can instantly select words for practice on the approximate grade level of the child.

Suggestions are offered for supplementary drill, according to the pupil's need. Through the use of the word lists, types of practice sentences, and a loose leaf notebook, an almost inexhaustible supply of practice exercises may be had.

Poems, classified according to the sound for which they provide repetition, range in interest from the Kindergarten and Primary Level to the Junior High School.

II. Articulation Test Material.

Diagnostic Sentences with *Key, Diagnostic Test Words, Phonovisual Diagnostic Consonant and Vowel Charts,* and a *Diagnostic Chart* offer an easy method of identifying the consonant and vowel errors which appear in a pupil's speech. (See page 138.) The *Key to the Sentences* indicates the consonant and vowel sounds to be tested. The *Diagnostic Chart* is used to record the results of the Test. It also provides space for a brief case history.

III. Tongue and Lip Exercises.

Tongue and Lip Exercises have been selected, which, if practised regularly, will give strength and flexibility and make for more normal, distinct speech.

IV. *Drill Words.*

Drill words are given for each consonant and vowel, as well as for the consonant blends. The *Table of Contents* indicates the order in which the consonants and vowels appear. They are grouped and classified according to *A Guide to Pronunciation, Merriam-Webster New International Dictionary—Second Edition.* Consonant blends are arranged alphabetically in the groups for which they provide practice.

An alphabetical index of drills for both consonants and vowels may be found on page 217. A key to the vowels is given on page 134.

The word lists in each group, while not exhaustive, are as comprehensive as possible in a book of this type. The pupil should be encouraged to list similar words in his Work Book. For further suggestions, see "Meeting the Needs of the Individual with a Work Book," page xv.

V. *Practice Sentences.*

Following each group of drill words, practice sentences based on the word lists are provided. In some instances, the combined sentences in a group tell a short story. The completion type of sentence has been included to lend variety to the practice exercises. Through the use of the Work Book additional sentences based on the word lists may be written by the pupil or provided by the teacher on the appropriate grade level. See page xv.

VI. *Poems.*

Experience proves that *once a pupil has mastered the elementary sounds,* he acquires the habit of correct speaking more easily by memorizing verses than by the repetition of words and sentences. The poems in this book have been carefully selected for their rhythm, charm, and appeal to children, as well as for their repetition of certain sounds. They are classified under the sounds for which they provide practice. A word of caution is given lest the teacher mar the charm of the poem by emphasizing too greatly the repetition of the sound upon which the pupil is working. Speech correction pupils should list all words in the poem for practice before reading the poem aloud. These should be *thoroughly* mastered before the poem is read aloud.

These poems, ranging in grade from the Kindergarten to Junior High, have an almost universal appeal to children. Their use is suggested with the hope that a child, through his natural love of poetry, will find renewed interest and joy in perfecting his speech.

MEETING THE NEEDS OF THE INDIVIDUAL—WITH A WORK BOOK

However complete a textbook may be, there are times when the exercises must be adapted to individual needs. For this reason it is recommended that the pupil be provided with a loose-leaf notebook which may be used as a Work Book. This makes possible the easy adaptation of the exercises in *Better Speech and Better Reading* to pupils of varying abilities and different learning levels.

Suggestions for Using the Work Book

After the pupil has practised the word lists and sentences *on his own grade level* in *Better Speech and Better Reading*, he may use the work book as follows for:

1. **Practice Words**

    a. Additional words containing the designated sound may be dictated by the teacher, and written and practiced by the pupil.
    b. The pupil may be encouraged to think of additional words and bring in a list for practice in the class.
    c. Older pupils may find additional practice words in the dictionary.

2. **Practice Sentences**

    a. Pupils may write in their work books additional sentences based on the word lists from *Better Speech and Better Reading*, or from their own word lists. Through the contributions of a class much interesting material may be gathered and much pleasure experienced by the competitors.

3. **Practice in the Pupil's Own Reader**

    a. A page from the pupil's own reader should be selected. The pupil should list all words on the page which contain the designated sound. The page should not be read aloud until the listed words are spoken smoothly and correctly.

4. **Poems for Practice**

    a. The pupil should choose a poem from *Better Speech and Better Reading*, and should list all words in the poem which contain the designated sound. These words should be thoroughly mastered before the entire poem is studied. See page xiv.
    b. The pupil should be urged to select poems from his own reading, and incorporate them in his work book. Many of the poems in *Better Speech and Better Reading* were brought in by pupils who, in searching for particular sounds, found poems which delighted them and furnished the best kind of motivation for perfecting their speech. Further interest is often stimulated if the pupil is encouraged to illustrate the poem.

DIAGNOSTIC SENTENCES
AND
DIAGNOSTIC TEST WORDS

DIAGNOSTIC SENTENCES*

Read these sentences aloud:

1. The girl put the paper on top of the table.
2. The boy put the baby in the tub.
3. The man saw the farmer at the farm.
4. Please put the wheel somewhere else.
5. We are going away on Monday.
6. The farmer has a beautiful calf.
7. The village by the river is five miles away.
8. I think his birthday is next month.
9. That mother will go with her son.
10. I told her your letter had not come.
11. Twenty boys stood between the houses.
12. Did Daddy ride the horse?
13. The dwarf lives in the wood.
14. Do not give money to that man.
15. A lady gave us the tulips in that bowl.
16. The black bunny is nibbling a carrot.
17. The clown declared he was sick.
18. The flying snowflakes are beautiful.
19. I am glad my looking-glass wasn't broken.
20. Please look at the airplane I made.
21. The sly boy seemed to be asleep.
22. The baby splashed in her tub.

* For the identification of consonant and vowel errors in speech. See page 138.

23. The baby is in the cradle.
24. The boy caught a turtle.
25. He has a new puzzle.
26. The rabbit ate a carrot.
27. Bring your umbrella with you.
28. She heard the baby crying across the road.
29. Please draw a picture for the children.
30. My friend is not afraid.
31. Grandma gives me cake when I am hungry.
32. The prince surprised the king.
33. She screamed when he described the fight.
34. We have some shrubs in our yard.
35. I like the spring of the year.
36. The street car destroyed the bicycle.
37. I shall try to go to the country on Monday.
38. He has three books for you.
39. I saw the policeman near our house.
40. The school basket is by my desk.
41. I saw the smoke.
42. I like to play in the snow.
43. Although I spoke in a whisper it made her gasp.
44. He stayed upstairs in the guest room.
45. Swing high, swing low, and over you'll go.
46. When she reads that story, she laughs.

47. No one else will be here.
48. She saw him only once.
49. Where are the blue cups?
50. Mary has two new hats.
51. Daddy has two white vests.
52. Were you away the last two months?
53. Zell came Thursday with the boys.
54. Look at the spider webs.
55. He has many friends.
56. Where are the other girls?
57. Did you bring both drums?
58. I play in the house when it rains.
59. We learned two new songs.
60. He tore his clothes.
61. I will show you where Bob lives.
62. I shall sit in the sunshine near the bush.
63. Father put his car as usual in our garage.
64. The child saw his teacher in church.
65. Jack has a pigeon in a cage.
66. Do you like onions?
67. Come and see the monkey in my book.
68. After milking the cow put the milk in the can.
69. The queen requested the king to see the man.
70. The squirrel is in the cage.

71. All the boys are here except Max.
72. We shall go in the wagon to get the dog.
73. Those are exactly the right flags.
74. She was swinging in our swing.
75. He hid behind the house.
76. He saw a sheep asleep in the field.
77. Did you buy the ring in our city?
78. The little red hen laid an egg in the nest.
79. There is the best chair for Baby Bear.
80. That fat man looks very happy.
81. She cut the bread and buttered it for lunch.
82. Her bird was hurt when the cage turned over.
83. He paid about a dollar for his dog's collar.
84. He drew a picture of the stool in our room.
85. She put the book where he could see it.
86. Dan caught all the horses in the cornfield.
87. Do not drop the hot porridge.
88. How far is your garden from our barn?
89. They came on the train the other day.
90. My child will be five by the time school opens.
91. It is so cold I hope you will wear your coat.
92. How did you get the cat out of the house?
93. The boy soiled his hands with oil.
94. Hugh has a beautiful tulip.

DIAGNOSTIC TEST WORDS.[1]

Read these words aloud:

1.	pie	up		7.	very	have
	put	keep			voice	give
	pig	top			visit	five
2.	be	rub		8.	thank	mouth
	boy	web			think	bath
	but	tub			thing	both
3.	me	am		9.	the	with
	my	him			they	smooth
	man	name			that	bathe
4.	why	—		10.	too	at
	when	—			tell	put
	white	—			toy	kite
5.	we	—		11.	twelve	—
	will	—			twenty	—
	was	—			twin	—
6.	farm	if		12.	do	red
	fire	off			doll	bad
	feet	wolf			dog	good

[1] For the identification of consonant and vowel errors in speech. See page 138 for use of *Diagnostic Test Words*. Note that this test is less complete than that given by the Diagnostic Sentences.

13.	dwarf	—		19.	glad	—
	dwell	—			glass	—
	dwelt	—			gloves	—
14.	no	sun		20.	play	—
	not	ten			please	—
	now	man			plant	—
15.	lay	all		21.	sled	—
	let	pull			sleep	—
	leg	girl			slow	—
16.	blue	—		22.	splash	—
	black	—			splendid	—
	block	—			split (23–25)	—
17.	clock	—		26.	ran	—
	climb	—			red	—
	clean	—			rope	—
18.	fly	—		27.	bring	—
	flag	—			bread	—
	floor	—			broom	—

28.	cry	—	34.	*shrub	—
	crayon	—		*shrug	
	cradle	—		*shred	—
29.	draw	—	35.	spring	—
	drink	—		spread	—
	dress	—		sprang	—
30.	from	—	36.	street	—
	friend	—		string	—
	frog	—		strong	—
31.	green	—	37.	tree	—
	great	—		try	—
	grow	—		train	—
32.	pretty	—	38.	three	—
	present	—		throw	—
	prince	—		through	—
33.	scream	—	39.	saw	us
	scrub	—		see	house
	scratch	—		said	horse

* Not in Gates or Thorndike Primary Word Lists.

DIAGNOSTIC TEST WORDS—continued

40.	sky	ask
	skate	desk
	skip	dusk

41.	small	—
	smile	—
	smoke	—

42.	snow	—
	snake	—
	snap	—

43.	spoon	—
	speak	—
	spin	—

44.	star	nest
	stand	must
	stay	best

45.	swim	—
	sweet	—
	swing	—

(46–52)

53.	zoo	is
	zebra	his
	zone	was

(54–61)

62.	shoe	wish
	ship	dish
	shall	fish

(63)

64.	chair	much
	child	which
	chick	watch

65.	jump	age
	just	cage
	jar	large

66.	you	—
	yes	—
	your	—

67.	keep	cook
	kite	cake
	kind	book

(68)

69.	queen	—	76.	he	eat
	quick	—		see	seat
	quiet	—		seed	meat

70.	squirrel	—	77.	sit	did
	square	—		hit	big
	squeeze	—		his	pig

71.	—	box	78.	met	said
	—	fox		get	head
	—	six		leg	bread

72.	go	big	79.	hair	bear
	good	pig		chair	pear
	gate	leg		fair	care

(73)

74.	—	sing	80.	cat	bad
	—	thing		hat	had
	—	long		that	has

75.	he	—	81.	cup	sun
	hop	—		cut	fun
	hot	—		but	nut

82.	turn	bird	89.	make	may
	burn	heard		cake	say
	hurt	work		came	paint
(83)					
84.	moon	do	90.	mice	by
	soon	who		like	my
	soup	shoe		kite	tie
85.	book	could	91.	go	goat
	cook	would		gold	boat
	look	should		cold	coat
86.	horn	saw	92.	mouse	cow
	horse	paw		house	now
	corn	walk		mouth	how
87.	not	top	93.	boy	noise
	got	stop		toy	voice
	hot	hop		joy	boil
88.	car	are	94.	new	use
	far	arm		mew	cube
	star	farm		few	cute

Phonovisual Consonant Chart*

p— b— m-

wh. w— qu-

f— v—
ph

3 th- this th-

t— d— n— l—

s— z— r—
c   s

sh- y—

ch- j—
tch   g

k— g— -ng -x
c   n(k)
ck

h—

*See p. 12

Phonovisual Vowel Chart*

a–e
ay
ai

ee
-e
ea

5
i–e
-y
igh

o–e
oa
ow
–o

u–e
ew

-a-

-e-
ea

-i-
–y

-o-

-u-

aw
au
a(ll)
o(r)

oo

ur
er
ir
or

a(r)

oo
u

ow
ou

oy
oi

*See p. 12

THE PHONOVISUAL CHARTS*

"The Phonovisual Charts (pages 11a and 11b) are a part of the Phonovisual Method of teaching better reading, better spelling, and better speech. They contain all the elements of speech, which the normal child learns in babyhood during the babbling period. As is well known, a child speaks English because he hears English, Dutch because he hears Dutch, French because he hears French. He does not begin to speak in words, but babbles consonant and vowel sounds months before he combines them to make words.

"It seems probable that the child with defective speech has heard certain sounds incorrectly, not because he is hard of hearing, but because he may be lacking in the finer powers of auditory discrimination. The training provided by the Phonovisual Method automatically corrects many defective speech sounds without the necessity for laborious teaching and prolonged speech drills."*

THE USE OF THE PHONOVISUAL CHARTS FOR DIAGNOSING SPEECH DEFECTS

These charts may be used to test the child who has not yet learned to read. Only the initial sound is tested, except final ng and x. The index numbers on the charts correspond to the numbers on the Articulation Test of the Speech Diagnostic Chart (page 140). The teacher should first name each picture on the Consonant Chart to be sure the child identifies it correctly. Then the pupil should be asked to name each picture. The teacher should record the errors made on the Articulation Test as noted in paragraph 3, page 138. Proceed in the same way with the Vowel Chart.

---

* Reproduced here by courtesy of Phonovisual Products, Inc., Box 5625, Washington 16, D. C. Individual charts (8½" x 11") and large charts (25" x 38"), both printed in color, together with the Phonovisual Method Book, are obtainable either from the Expression Company or from Phonovisual Products.

PRACTICE EXERCISES

I. For Strengthening the Organs of Speech

        Tongue Exercises

        Lip Exercises

TONGUE EXERCISES

Practice these exercises each day, if you wish your speech to improve. Do them just as regularly as you would other gymnastic exercises. Repeat each exercise at least three times. If you find one exercise more difficult than another, practice it until you can do it easily.

1. **Point your tongue. Draw it in and close your lips. 1—2; 1—2; 1—2; 1—2.**

(Explanation: On the count of 1, stretch your tongue out as far as possible. Do not let it touch your lips or teeth. On the count of 2, draw it in and close your lips. Throughout all these exercises, always close your lips on the count of 2.)

2. **Stretch your tongue up. 1—2; 1—2; 1—2.**

(Explanation: On the count of 1, stretch your tongue up. Try to touch your nose. On the count of 2, remember to draw your tongue in and close your lips.)

3. **Stretch your tongue down. 1—2; 1—2; 1—2.**

(Explanation: On the count of 1, stretch your tongue down. Try to touch your chin. On the count of 2, draw it in and close your lips.)

4. **Press your tongue against your upper gums. 1-2; 1—2; 1—2.**

(Explanation: Open your mouth wide on the count of 1, and place the tip of your tongue against your gums just above your upper teeth. Press *hard* until you can feel the strength in the tip. On the count of 2, close your lips.)

5. **Press your tongue against your lower gums. 1—2; 1—2; 1—2.**

(Explanation: Same as exercise 4, except your tongue is against your lower gums instead of your upper gums. Remember to press *hard*.)

6. **Roll the tip of your tongue against your upper teeth.**

(Explanation: Roll the tip of your tongue so that the under side protrudes. Close your teeth gently on your tongue. Rest. Repeat.)

7. **Roll the tip of your tongue against your lower teeth. Blow over the center.**

(Explanation: Roll the tip of the tongue against your lower teeth. Flatten your tongue, keeping the tip rolled. Then blow through the center. Rest. Repeat.)

8. **Widen your tongue against your upper gums.**

(Explanation: Place the tip of your tongue against your upper gum. Widen your tongue so that it extends beyond the teeth. Then narrow it. Repeat several times.)

9. **Widen your tongue against your lower gums.**

(Explanation: Let your tongue lie flat in your mouth with the tip against the lower gum; widen, then narrow your tongue. Repeat.)

10. **Groove your tongue. Blow through center.**

(Explanation: Protrude your tongue. Make a deep groove in your tongue by raising both sides. Hold the sides up with your teeth, if possible. Blow through center.)

11. **Say en—en—en—en—en.**

(Explanation: Say en, emphasizing this sound until you can feel the sides of your tongue pressed firmly against your upper teeth. Say en—en—en, making a humming noise by raising and lowering the tip of your tongue, without changing the positions of its sides.)

12. **Whistle over the tip of your tongue.**

(Explanation: With your lips spread apart and the sides of your tongue held against your upper gums and teeth try to give a sharp whistle over the tip of your tongue. Try sounding t-t-t-t-t- rapidly, prolonging the last sound into a sharp whistle.)

LIP EXERCISES

1. **Pucker your lips, pushing them as far forward as possible. Draw them back as far as possible.**

2. **Say "ee" pulling the lips back as far as possible. Say "oo" pushing the lips forward.**

(Explanation: These sounds should be greatly exaggerated. Repeat several times.)

3. **Open your mouth wide. Close your lips firmly. 1—2; 1—2; 1—2.**

(Explanation: On the count of 1, open your mouth wide. On the count of 2, close your lips.)

4. **Raise your upper lip showing your upper front teeth. Close your lips. 1—2; 1—2; 1—2.**

(Explanation: You can raise your upper lip by wrinkling up your nose.)

NOTE: The "explanations" given below the exercises are for the use of the teacher, primarily. After the pupil has practiced each exercise under the direction of his teacher, he needs only to read the directions in large type to perform the exercise.

PRACTICE EXERCISES

II. For the Consonants

p DRILLS FOR SOUND OF P

Webster: p
I.P.A.: [p]

1. Word Drill for p Sound

Say the following slowly. Listen for the p sound.

Initial	pl-	Medial	-lp
pie	play	papa	help
paw	place	paper	*pulp
pay	please	puppy	*scalp
paid	**pr-**	supper	**-mp**
paint	pray	suppose	jump
page	proud	happy	lump
pat	prince	pumpkin	lamp
pass	prize	upon	camp
pan	**sp-**	**Final**	**-sp**
pen	spoon	up	*clasp
penny	spin	cup	*grasp
pencil	spill	top	*crisp
pet	**spl-**	hop	**-ps**
pig	splash	lap	caps
pick	splendid	lip	cups
pink	*split	skip	tops
park	**spr-**	ship	**-pt**
poor	spring	sheep	kept
put	sprang	keep	crept
pull	spread	peep	slept

* Not in Gates or Thorndike Primary Word Lists.
NOTE: For additional "p" blends, consult page 217.

2. Practice Sentences for p Sound

Find the words in these sentences which contain the p sound. Read the sentences aloud slowly and carefully.

1. Did you pay a penny for your pen?

2. Paul paid a penny for his pencil.

3. Papa gave Paul some paints and paper.

4. Paul painted a picture of a puppy.

5. Peter painted a picture of a top.

6. Paul plays with the puppy after supper.

7. The puppy runs and jumps in the park.

3. Completion Game for p Sound

Read the beginning of the sentence. Find the word in the group which completes the sentence correctly.

1. Paul's pencil cost

     one puppy   one paper   one penny

2. After supper Paul plays with

     the paper   the puppy   the apron

3. The picture painted by Peter was

     a cup   a top   a lip

Write some additional sentences which contain the p sound in your Work Book. The word lists on the opposite page will help you.

4. Poems Containing the p Sound[1]

You will enjoy the poems in Group 1, page 148. Choose a poem to learn and recite to the class.

---

[1] For use of poems, consult *Plan of the Book*, page XIV.

b

DRILLS FOR SOUND OF B

Webster: b
I.P.A.: [b]

1. Word Drill for b Sound

Say the following words slowly. Listen for the b sound.

Initial	bl-[1]	Medial	Final
be	blue	baby	Bob
by	black	maybe	sob
boy	block	good-by	web
bear	blow	rock-a-by	tub
bad	blew	rabbit	rub
bag	bloom	cabbage	scrub
back	blame	somebody	crab
bath	blind	nobody	*grab
bed	blood	neighbor	*cab
bird	bless	number	*rob
big	**br-[2]**	rubber	*job
been	brown	October	*mob
ball	bread	November	*cob
bell	bring	December	*knob
boat	brought	remember	*bib
both	bright	about	*rib
but	broom	above	*robe
bug	branch	robin	*globe
buzz	break	bluebird	*grub
book	brave	blackbird	*cube

* Not in Gates or Thorndike Primary Word Lists.
[1] See also page 46.   [2] See also page 56.

2. Practice Sentences for b Sound

Find the words in these sentences which contain the b sound. Read the sentences aloud slowly and carefully.

1. Ben is a big boy.

2. Bob is a baby boy.

3. Ben has a baseball.

4. Bob has a rubber ball.

5. Bob likes to take a bath.

6. He plays with the ball in the tub.

7. "Rub-a-dub-dub," says Bob in the tub.

3. Completion Game for b Sound

Read the beginning of the sentence. Find the word in the group which completes the sentence correctly.

1. Ben is a
   bug   boat   boy

2. Bob's ball is made of
   cabbage   robin   rubber

3. Bob took a bath in the
   tub   rub   web

Write some additional sentences which contain the b sound in your Work Book. The word lists on the opposite page will help you.

4. Poems Containing the b Sound[1]

You will enjoy the poems in Group 2, page 151. Choose a poem to learn and recite to the class.

---

[1] For use of poems, consult *Plan of the Book*, page XIV.

m   DRILLS FOR SOUND OF M   Webster: m
I.P.A.: [m]

1. Word Drill for m Sound

Say the following words slowly. Listen for the m sound.

Initial	Medial	Final	Final
me	mamma	am	from
my	summer	arm	drum
may	hammer	farm	plum
make	coming	harm	swim
made	among	him	swam
man	animal	whom	bloom
men	fireman	room	broom
met	milkman	seem	dream
meat	family	same	cream
moon	company	name	scream
mice	number	game	stream
miss	moment	tame	storm
more	someone	came	**-lm**
most	somewhere	come	*elm
must	chipmunk	some	*helm
milk	remember	time	*realm
sm-[1]	November	home	**-sm(-zm)**
smile	December	hum	*heroism
smell	Christmas	gum	*criticism
small	America	them	*enthusiasm

---

* Not in Gates or Thorndike Primary Word Lists.
[1] See also page 73.

2. Practice Sentences for m Sound

Can you find the words in these sentences which contain the m sound?
Read the sentences aloud slowly and carefully.

1. "Good morning, Mother," said Mary.

2. "Good morning, Mary," said Mother.

3. May I get the milk from the milkman?

4. The milkman came sometime ago.

5. Are you going to the farm with me?

6. The farmer's name is Mr. March.

7. May I see some of the animals on the farm?

3. Completion Game for m Sound

Read the beginning of the sentence.   Find the word in the group which
completes the sentence correctly.

1. Mary said good morning to
   mouse   mother   Mr. March

2. Mr. March is a
   fireman   policeman   farmer

3. Mr. March has a
   farm   drum   cream

Write some additional sentences which contain the m sound in your Work
Book.   The word lists on the opposite page will help you.

4. Poems Containing the m Sound[1]

You will enjoy the poems in Group 3, page 153.   Choose a poem to learn
and recite to the class.

---

[1] For use of poems, consult *Plan of the Book*, page XIV.

wh

DRILLS FOR SOUND OF Wh

Webster: hw
I.P.A.: [hw]

1. Word Drill for wh Sound

Say the following words slowly.   Listen for the wh sound.

Initial	Initial	Medial
what	whatever	somewhat
when	whenever	somewhere
where	wherever	everywhere
which	whirl	nowhere
why	whale	anywhere
while	wharf	*elsewhere
whine	whip	*awhile
white	whiz	*meanwhile
wheat	whisper	*pinwheel
wheel	whistle	*bobwhite
wheelbarrow	*whittle	*overwhelm

---

* Not in Gates or Thorndike Primary Word Lists.

2. Practice Sentences for wh Sound

Find the words in these sentences which contain the wh sound. Read the sentences aloud slowly and carefully.

1. Where did you find the white whistle?

2. Which whistle is yours?

3. Which whip is yours?

4. Where did you go on your wheel?

5. I rode everywhere on my wheel.

6. Why did you whisper to her?

7. The bobwhite flew everywhere in the wheat field.

3. Completion Game for wh Sound

Read the beginning of the sentence. Find the word in the group which completes the sentence correctly.

1. You can blow a
   whistle   wheat   white

2. A wagon has four
   wheat   wheels   whales

3. The bobwhite flew over the
   while   white   wheat

Write some additional sentences which contain the wh sound in your Work Book. The word lists on the opposite page will help you.

4. Poems Containing the wh Sound[1]

You will enjoy the poems in Group 4, page 154. Choose a poem to learn and recite to the class.

---

[1] For use of poems, consult *Plan of the Book*, page XIV.

DRILLS FOR SOUND OF W

1. Word Drill for w Sound

Say the following words slowly.   Listen for the w sound.

Initial	Initial	dw-	Medial
we	week	dwarf	away
wee	wake	dwell	awake
way	wait	*dwelt	awoke
were	wear	*dwelling	always
was	wore	*dwindle	bowwow
well	wall	**qu-(kw-)**[1]	wigwam
wet	walk	queen	sidewalk
west	wash	quiet	sandwich
web	watch	**squ-(skw-)**[1]	anyway
went	warm	square	someway
win	water	squirrel	highway
wind	wade	**sw-**[1]	following
window	wave	sweet	otherwise
winter	wag	swing	afterward
with	wagon	**tw-**	backward
wish	wise	twelve	eastward
witch	wife	twenty	westward
work	wide	twin	anyone
word	wire	twinkle	someone
wood	wolf	twig	everyone

* Not in Gates or Thorndike Primary Word Lists.
[1] For additional "w" blends, consult page 217.

2. Practice Sentences for w Sound

Find the words in these sentences which contain the w sound. Read the sentences aloud slowly and carefully.

1.   We went away last week.

2.   We went to see Uncle William.

3.   Uncle William has a wagon.

4.   We rode with him to work.

5.   We went to the woods.

6.   We filled the wagon with wood.

7.   Afterwards we ate sandwiches.

3. Completion Game for w Sound

Read the beginning of the sentence. Find the word in the group which completes the sentence correctly.

1.   We went for a ride in Uncle William's
     window   wagon   watch

2.   The wagon was filled
     with water   with words   with wood

3.   After filling the wagon we ate
     wigwams   sandwiches   sidewalks

Write some additional sentences which contain the w sound in your Work Book. The word lists on the opposite page will help you.

4. Poems Containing the w Sound[1]

You will enjoy the poems in Group 4, page 154. Choose a poem to learn and recite to the class.

---

[1] For use of poems, consult *Plan of the Book*, page XIV.

f

DRILLS FOR SOUND OF F

1. Word Drill for f Sound

Say the following words slowly.   Listen for the f sound.

Initial	fl-[1]	Medial	Final
far	fly	before	if
farm	flies	after	off
farmer	flew	afternoon	leaf
four	flow	beautiful	loaf
fun	floor	wonderful	life
fine	float	careful	knife
find	flag	goldfish	wife
fire	flat	elephant	safe
fish	flower	telephone	roof
fill	**fr-[2]**	laughing	puff
fell	free	coughing	laugh
feel	friend	breakfast	cough
field	from	coffee	wolf
feed	frog	office	self
feet	frost	safely	**-ft**
foot	fresh	softly	soft
fast	fruit	selfish	left
for	frank	butterfly	lift
fork	Friday	snowflake	gift

NOTE: The teacher should explain that *other spellings* represent the sound of *f* as in *far*, for example: lau*gh*, tele*ph*one.
[1] See also page 48.   [2] See also page 59.

2. Practice Sentences for f Sound

Find the words in these sentences which contain the f sound.   Read the sentences aloud slowly and carefully.

1.   Fan's home is on a farm.

2.   Her father is a farmer.

3.   Fan has fun on the farm.

4.   She finds beautiful flowers in the field.

5.   She sees the butterflies on the flowers.

6.   Fred found a fine knife in the field.

7.   Fan left it there.   She forgot it.

3. Completion Game for f Sound

Read the beginning of the sentence.   Find the word in the group which completes the sentence correctly.

1.   Fan lives with her father
     on a fork   on a farm   on a fish

2.   Fan was in the field and saw some
     goldfish   butterflies   snowflakes

3.   Fred was in the field and found a
     leaf   wife   knife   wolf

Write some additional sentences which contain the f sound in your Work Book.   The word lists on the opposite page will help you.

4. Poems Containing the f Sound[1]

You will enjoy the poems in Group 5, page 157.   Choose a poem to learn and recite to the class.

---

[1] For use of poems, consult *Plan of the Book*, page XIV.

V # DRILLS FOR SOUND OF V

1. Word Drill for v Sound

Say the following words slowly. Listen for the v sound.

Initial	Medial	Final
very	ever	have
visit	never	gave
village	every	give
Virginia	over	live
view	clover	love
vine	river	glove
violet	cover	above
valentine	evening	dove
valley	invite	five
value	divide	dive
vegetable	heavy	move
vessel	seventy	save
vest	lovely	cave
voice	servant	brave
various	velvet	slave
vain	even	wave
vote	given	wove
*vow	seven	stove
*vex	eleven	leave
*vein	heaven	twelve

* Not in Gates or Thorndike Primary Word Lists.

2. Practice Sentences for v Sound

Find the words in these sentences which contain the v sound. Read the sentences aloud slowly and carefully.

1. Virginia is visiting Dot.

2. Dot lives in a village.

3. The village is near the river.

4. Dot and Virginia go to the river every evening.

5. Virginia gave Dot a valentine.

6. The valentine said, "I love you."

7. Dot received seven valentines.

3. Completion Game for v Sound

Read the beginning of the sentence. Find the word in the group which completes the sentence correctly.

1. Virginia went to visit in a

     violet   valentine   village

2. Dot's home is near the

     clover   river   velvet

3. Dot was given seven

     valleys   villages   valentines

Write some additional sentences which contain the v sound in your Work Book. The word lists on the opposite page will help you.

4. Poems Containing the v Sound[1]

You will enjoy the poems in Group 6, page 158. Choose a poem to learn and recite to the class.

---

[1] For use of poems, consult *Plan of the Book*, page XIV.

th DRILLS FOR SOUNDS OF Th

Webster: th
I.P.A.: [θ]

1. Word Drill for Voiceless th Sound

Say the following words.   Listen for the voiceless th sound.

Initial	thr-[1]	Final	Final
thank	three	both	earth
think	throw	bath	worth
thick	threw	path	birth
thin	through	south	north
thing	thread	mouth	health
thought	throat	cloth	wealth
thousand	*throne	teeth	month
third	*thrust	tooth	length
thirty	**Medial**	youth	strength
Thursday	nothing	truth	fourth
thirsty	anything	Ruth	fifth
*thirst	something	Beth	*sixth
*thirteen	plaything	death	*seventh
*thumb	healthy	breath	*eighth
*thump	birthday	faith	*ninth
*thunder	faithful	*moth	*tenth
*thimble	method	*broth	*eleventh
*thigh	Kathleen	*growth	*twelfth
*thorn	Arthur	*oath	*width
*thief	author	*hath	*breadth

* Not in Gates or Thorndike Primary Word Lists.   [1] See also page 63.

2. Practice Sentences for Voiceless th Sound

Find the words in these sentences which contain the voiceless th sound. Read the sentences aloud slowly and carefully.

1. Do you think we can have our picnic Thursday?

2. I think Thursday will be fine.

3. Shall I take anything for lunch?

4. No, thank you, Arthur will take everything.

5. I thought Arthur was in the South.

6. He came back from the South on the third.

7. Are Ruth and Beth going?

8. Yes, it is Ruth's birthday.

9. We will take a birthday cake for Ruth.

3. Completion Game for Voiceless th Sound

Find the right word to complete the sentence.

1. Our picnic will be
    thirty   thirsty   Thursday

2. Thursday will be Ruth's
    plaything   birthday   everything

3. Arthur took a trip to the
    month   South   tooth

Write some additional sentences, which contain the voiceless th sound, in your Work Book. The word lists on the opposite page will help you.

4. Word Drill for Voiced th Sound

Say the following words.   Listen for the voiced th sound.

Initial	Medial	Final
the	other	with
they	another	smooth
them	mother	bathe
then	brother	breathe
there	father	clothe
their	feather	*booth
this	together	*soothe
that	weather	*seethe
than	leather	*wreathe
though	further	*writhe
those	either	*scythe
these	neither	*blithe
thus	gather	*tithe
thou	rather	*lathe
thy	although	*loathe
*thine	within	*bequeath

* Not in Gates or Thorndike Primary Word Lists.

5. Practice Sentences for Voiced th Sound

Find the words in these sentences which contain the voiced th sound. Read the sentences aloud slowly and carefully.

1. The boys went down that road.

2. They went to see their grandmother.

3. They will meet their father there.

4. They will all drive home together.

5. Ted, the younger brother, stayed with his mother.

6. Their father has a pair of leather boots.

7. He wears his leather boots in wet weather.

6. Completion Game for Voiced th Sound

Read the beginning of the sentence. Find the word in the group which completes the sentence correctly.

1. The boys went to see their
   feather   grandmother   father

2. They drove home in a car with
   their feather   the weather   their father

3. Ted's father wears boots made of
   feather   leather   another

Write some additional sentences which contain the voiced th sound in your Work Book. The word lists on the opposite page will help you.

7. Poems Containing the th Sound[1]

You will enjoy the poems in Group 7, page 160. Choose a poem to learn and recite to the class.

---

[1] For use of poems, consult *Plan of the Book*, page XIV.

t

DRILLS FOR SOUND OF T

Webster: t
I.P.A.: [t]

1. Word Drill for t Sound

Say the following words slowly. Listen for the t sound.

Initial	Medial	Final	-ct (-ked)
to	into	it	act
toe	after	hit	waked
toy	butter	at	baked
top	better	cat	**-cht (-ched)**
tie	letter	cut	touched
time	lettuce	coat	reached
ten	potato	goat	marched
town	until	got	**-pt (-ped)**
take	city	not	kept
took	pretty	hot	crept
tell	dirty	kite	dropped
tall	party	gate	snapped
tr-[1]	naughty	late	**-sht (-shed)**
try	sometime	left	washed
tree	valentine	soft	wished
train	beautiful	salt	fished
tw-	yesterday	want	**-xt (-xed)**
twelve	sister	went	next
twenty	chapter	west	fixed
twin	daughter	last	mixed

[1] See also page 62.

2. Practice Sentences for t Sound

Find the words in these sentences which contain the t sound. Read the sentences aloud slowly and carefully.

1. Please tell me about Tom.

2. Tom is our big white cat.

3. Tom is Ted's pet.

4. One day Ted took Tom to town.

5. Tom got lost.

6. Tom walked two miles to get home.

7. Tom was tired and hot and dirty.

3. Completion Game for t Sound

Read the beginning of the sentence. Find the word in the group which completes the sentence correctly.

1. Ted took Tom to
   ten   town   time

2. Tom got tired and
   pretty   better   dirty

3. Tom is a big
   coat   cut   cat

Write some additional sentences which contain the t sound in your Work Book. The word lists on the opposite page will help you.

4. Poems Containing the t Sound[1]

You will enjoy the poems in Group 8, page 164. Choose a poem to learn and recite to the class.

---

[1] For use of poems, consult *Plan of the Book*, page XIV.

d DRILLS FOR SOUND OF D

Webster: d
I.P.A.: [d]

1. Word Drill for d Sound

Say the following words slowly. Listen for the d sound.

Initial	Medial	Final	Final
do	daddy	did	used
day	lady	dead	loved
dear	today	head	rubbed
door	Monday	red	sobbed
dark	candy	had	bobbed
doll	ready	bad	robbed
dog	birdie	bed	begged
dig	meadow	bird	hugged
dish	window	mud	dragged
duck	indeed	made	roomed
does	under	and	seemed
done	wonder	sand	dreamed
down	nobody	hand	changed
desk	somebody	old	bathed
dr-[1]	reindeer	cold	clothed
draw	Indian	gold	moved
dry	spider	hold	saved
dw-[2]	radish	told	raised
dwarf	children	child	praised
dwell	hundred	cried	buzzed

[1] See also page 58.   [2] See also page 26.

2. Practice Sentences for d Sound

Find the words in these sentences which contain the d sound. Read the sentences aloud slowly and carefully.

1. Dorothy has a Dutch doll.
2. Daddy gave the doll to Dorothy.
3. The doll has golden hair.
4. One day Dorothy dropped her doll in the mud.
5. The doll's dress was very dirty.
6. The golden hair was dirty.
7. Dorothy cried and cried and cried.

3. Completion Game for d Sound

Read the beginning of the sentence. Find the word in the group which completes the sentence correctly.

1. Dorothy's father gave her a
         dog   duck   dish   doll

2. Dorothy's doll is a
         duck doll   dark doll   Dutch doll

3. When Dorothy dropped her doll, she
         begged   bathed   cried   read

Write some additional sentences which contain the d sound in your Work Book. The word lists on the opposite page will help you.

4. Poems Containing the d Sound[1]

You will enjoy the poems in Group 9, page 165. Choose a poem to learn and recite to the class.

---

[1] For use of poems, consult *Plan of the Book*, page XIV.

n   # DRILLS FOR SOUND OF N
Webster: n
                                                     I.P.A.: [n]

1. Word Drill for <u>n</u> Sound

Say the following words slowly.   Listen for the <u>n</u> sound.

Initial	Medial	Final	Final
no	any	in	chicken
nose	many	an	kitten
nice	penny	on	mitten
night	pony	been	written
new	money	sun	listen
now	funny	run	lesson
not	teeny.	ran	happen
nut	tiny	can	garden
name	dinner	man	hidden
nail	enough	hen	sudden
neck	peanut	ten	open
nest	banana	rain	spoken
near	into	moon	broken
north	until	noon	ripen
need	under	nine	waken
neat	animal	fine	cotton
<u>**sn-**</u>[1]	window	down	fasten
snow	only	town	season
snap	cannot	burn	reason
snake	Indian	learn	cousin

[1] See also page 74.

2. Practice Sentences for n Sound

Find the words in these sentences which contain the n sound. Read the sentences aloud slowly and carefully.

1. Nan has a brother named Ned.

2. Ned has a dog named Rin-Tin-Tin.

3. Nan and Ned have a pony named Nellie.

4. Ned can ride the pony.

5. Rin-Tin-Tin jumps and runs after the pony.

6. Ned says, "Down, Rin-Tin-Tin, down!"

7. Nan and Ned have a cousin named Jane.

3. Completion Game for n Sound

Read the beginning of the sentence. Find the word in the group which completes the sentence correctly.

1. Nan's brother is named
   neat   Rin-Tin-Tin   Ned   nut

2. Nan and Ned like to ride
   on the penny   on a window   on a pony

3. Ned has a sister named
   Anne   Nellie   Minnie   Nan

Write some additional sentences which contain the n sound in your Work Book. The word lists on the opposite page will help you.

4. Poems Containing the n Sound[1]

You will enjoy the poems in Group 10, page 166. Choose a poem to learn and recite to the class.

---

[1] For use of poems, consult *Plan of the Book*, page XIV.

DRILLS FOR SOUND OF L

Webster: l
I.P.A.: [l]

1. Word Drill for l Sound

Say the following words slowly. Listen for the l sound.

Initial	Initial	Medial	Medial
lay	lamb	alone	also
late	lamp	along	always
lady	land	belong	almost
ladies	lap	below	although
lake	last	balloon	color
laid	laugh	tulip	collar
leaf	leg	dandelion	dollar
leaves	let	violet	yellow
leave	left	polite	fellow
lie	lift	eleven	follow
like	lip	only	hollow
light	live	family	valentine
line	log	hardly	telephone
lion	lock	easily	telling
low	long	lovely	selling
loaf	lot	lonely	falling
load	look	lily	willing
loud	love	silly	milkmen
loose	lunch	Billy	velvet
lose	learn	dolly	umbrella

2. Practice Sentences for l Sound

Find the words in these sentences which contain the l sound. Read the sentences aloud slowly and carefully.

1. Look at the baby lamb.

2. The lamb belongs to Louise.

3. The lamb likes to run on the lawn.

4. It likes to lie in the sun by the lake.

5. Louise loves the baby lamb.

6. Louise's brother Billy has a collie puppy.

7. The lamb and the collie lie on the lawn together.

8. They like to lie in the leaves.

9. The collie is larger than the baby lamb.

3. Completion Game for l Sound

Find the right word to complete the sentence.

1. The baby lamb belongs to
   lady   Louise   light

2. The collie belongs to
   Louise   Billy   dolly

3. The collie and the lamb lie
   in the lake   in the leaves   on a lion

Write some additional sentences which contain the l sound in your Work Book. The word lists on the opposite page will help you.

DRILLS FOR SOUND OF L—continued

4. Word Drill for <u>l</u> Sound—continued

Say the following words slowly.   Listen for the <u>l</u> sound.

<u>Final</u>	<u>Final</u>	<u>-ld</u>	<u>-ls</u>
all	able	old	else
ball	table	cold	*false
call	nibble	sold	<u>-ls (-lz)</u>
fall	bubble	hold	balls
tall	uncle	held	calls
tell	middle	child	dolls
bell	needle	<u>-lf</u>	pulls
well	cradle	elf	bowls
will	riddle	self	rolls
fill	fiddle	wolf	tells
mill	single	<u>-lk</u>	<u>-lt</u>
hill	eagle	milk	salt
hole	apple	silk	built
pull	people	*bulk	felt
full	purple	<u>-lm</u>	<u>-lth</u>
cool	little	elm	health
school	turtle	*film	wealth
girl	bottle	<u>-lp</u>	<u>-lv</u>
oil	gentle	help	twelve
owl	puzzle	*whelp	*shelve

* Not in Gates or Thorndike Primary Word Lists.

5. Completion Game for l Sound

Find the right word to complete the sentence.

tall.
1. I like to play   bell.
ball.

bell?
2. Will you let this girl ring the   ball?
doll?

owl.
3. We like to go to   bowl.
school.

full.
4. The ball rolled down the   hill.
tell.

ball.
5. The little child tried to roll the   fall.
tall.

cold.
6. This tall girl is eleven years   old.
told.

Write some additional sentences in your Work Book. The word lists on the opposite page will help you.

DRILLS FOR SOUND OF L—continued

6. bl[1]

Say these words slowly.   Listen for the l sound.

blue	bluebird	bless	*bliss
black	blackbird	blood	*blade
block	blackboard	bleed	*blaze
blossom	blackberry	blink	*blank
blew	blame	blind	*blanket
blow	bloom	*blond	*obliged

Find the bl words in these sentences.   Read the sentences aloud.

1. That block is blue.
2. This block is black.
3. My block is blue and black.
4. Color the large block blue.
5. Color the little block black.
6. Little Boy Blue, come blow your horn.
7. The wind blew and blew and blew.
8. The wind blew all the blossoms off the bush.
9. Dolly has a blue blanket.
10. A blackbird is on the blackberry bush.

Write some additional sentences in your Work Book using the above word lists.

---

* Not in Gates or Thorndike Primary Word Lists.   [1] See also page 20.

7. cl

Say these words slowly. Listen for the l sound.

clay	clap	claw	Santa Claus
cloud	class	cloth	o'clock
clown	clang	clear	declare
clean	cluck	clever	*decline
climb	clock	clover	*include
close	clothes	club	*incline

Find the cl words in these sentences. Read the sentences aloud.

1. Biddy Hen says, "Cluck! Cluck! Cluck!"
2. We saw a funny clown.
3. The clown tried to climb a pole.
4. The class clapped their hands.
5. The clown clucked like a hen.
6. He tore his clothes.
7. Santa Claus brought me a clown suit.
8. I wore my clown suit to school.
9. Our school opens at nine o'clock.
10. I have clean hands, a clean face, and clean clothes.

Write some additional sentences in your Work Book using the above word lists.

---

* Not in Gates or Thorndike Primary Word Lists.

8. fl[1]

Say these words slowly.   Listen for the l sound.

fly	flow	flea	*flame
flies	floor	flee	*flake
flying	flag	*fleet	*flock
flew	flap	*fleece	*float
flower	flash	*flesh	butterfly
flour	flat	*flood	snowflakes

Find the fl words in these sentences.   Read the sentences aloud.

1.   Fly, little bird, fly far away.

2.   Fly away, Jack!   Fly away, Jill!

3.   The little birds flew and flew and flew.

4.   The bees flew from flower to flower.

5.   The butterflies flew from flower to flower.

6.   Last winter the snowflakes were flying everywhere.

7.   The flag is flying from the pole.

8.   We salute our flag each morning.

9.   We never let our flag touch the floor.

10.   We think our flag is the best flag.

Write some additional sentences in your Work Book using the above word lists.

---

* Not in Gates or Thorndike Primary Word Lists.   [1] See also page 28.

9. gl[1]

Say these words slowly.   Listen for the l sound.

glass	*glassy	*glue	*glimmer
glad	*glare	*glow	*glimpse
glee	*gleam	*glorious	*glisten
glove	*glean	*globe	*glitter
gloves	*glen	*gloom	*glutton
glory	*glide	*gloomy	*aglow

Find the gl words in these sentences.   Read the sentences aloud.

1.   I am glad you came.

2.   I lost my glove on the way.

3.   May I have a glass of water?

4.   Billy would like a glass of milk.

5.   Will you lend me your looking-glass?

6.   I will gladly get the looking-glass for you.

7.   Let the baby look in the looking-glass.

8.   He is clapping his hands with glee.

9.   See how the glass glitters in the gleaming sun.

10.   I am glad to have this glimpse of you.

Write some additional sentences in your Work Book using the above word lists.

---

* Not in Gates or Thorndike Primary Word Lists.   [1] See also page 102.

10. pl

Say these words slowly.   Listen for the l sound.

			spl-[1]
play	playhouse	fireplace	
player	playmate	airplane	splash
place	plaything	reply	splendid
plate	plenty	replied	*splendor
plant	plow	*supply	*split
please	plum	*apply	*splinter

Find the pl words in these sentences.   Read the sentences aloud.

1.   Please, please, please come and play with me.

2.   We can play in my playhouse.

3.   I have some beautiful playthings.

4.   Do you like to play games?

5.   We can play the game of "Lotto."

6.   You may be the first player.

7.   Would you rather play with the airplane?

8.   Bob has an airplane that really flies.

9.   He let me play with it last summer.

10.   It flew away and splashed in the lake.

Write some additional sentences in your Work Book using the above word lists.

---

* Not in Gates or Thorndike Primary Word Lists.   [1] See also page 76.

DRILLS FOR SOUND OF L—continued

11. sl[1]

Say these words slowly. Listen for the l sound.

sly	sleigh	*sleet	*slang
slide	slip	*slid	*slant
sled	slipper	*slippery	*slander
sleep	slept	*slick	*slay
slow	*slope	*slit	*slayer
slowly	*slumber	*slim	asleep

Find the sl words in these sentences. Read the sentences aloud.

1. I have a new sled.
2. Will you let me slide on your sled?
3. My old sled is broken.
4. This hill looks very slippery.
5. Walk slowly, and do not slip.
6. The hill is covered with sleet.
7. It looks as slick as glass.
8. Louise slipped and hurt her leg.
9. I like to slide on a slippery hill.
10. I like to ride in a sleigh.

Write some additional sentences in your Work Book using the above word lists.

* Not in Gates or Thorndike Primary Word Lists.   [1] See also page 72.

12. Review Sentences for l Sound

Read these sentences aloud slowly and carefully.   Listen for the l sound.

1.   Louise and Laura are playmates.

2.   They like to play dolls in their playhouse.

3.   Santa Claus brought Louise a lovely doll.

4.   Laura has a Shirley Temple doll.

5.   Louise's doll has blue eyes.

6.   Laura's doll has a beautiful blue dress.

7.   Santa Claus came in a sleigh with jingling bells.

8.   Lewis bought a large yellow balloon for a nickel.

9.   Lewis likes to play baseball.

10.   He lost his baseball glove at school.

11.   Our school closes at twelve o'clock.

12.   The school clock was slow today.

13.   May I clean the blackboard with this old cloth?

14.   We salute our flag at school.

15.   The American flag is sometimes called "Old Glory."

13. Completion Game for l Sound

Find the right word to complete the sentence.

1. A lion has four
    lips   legs   lamps   lakes

2. A boy likes to play
    pull   call   ball   bell

3. You may color the balloon
    blow   blue   play   plow

4. I tell time by a
    glass   clown   clock   cluck

5. A butterfly can
    flag   flower   plow   fly

6. I like to slide on my
    sleep   cloud   sled   plate

7. Santa Claus comes in a
    clock   flower   glass   sleigh

Write some additional sentences in your Work Book.   Use as many words containing the l sound as possible.

14. Poems Containing the l Sound[1]

You will enjoy the poems in Group 11, page 167.   Choose a poem to learn and recite to the class.

---

[1] For use of poems, consult *Plan of the Book*, page XIV.

DRILLS FOR SOUND OF R

1. Word Drill for r Sound

Say the following words slowly.   Listen for the r sound.

Initial	Initial	Medial	Final[1]
ran	rake	around	are
rang	race	very	car
rat	raise	every	far
rabbit	rain	carry	air
radish	rainy	fairy	fair
rag	radio	story	hair
rap	read	furry	chair
red	reach	hurry	care
ready	real	marry	bear
rest	ride	married	pear
ring	right	sorry	or
rich	ripe	carrot	for
river	rice	arrow	four
ribbon	row	tomorrow	your
rock	rose	porridge	door
robin	roll	orange	dear
run	road	bedroom	near
rug	rope	terrible	ear
rub	room	squirrel	fire

[1] "Since speakers of some types of standard speech pronounce r where others do not" (See "A Guide to Pronunciation," Merriam-Webster), a list of final r words is given with the understanding that those who omit the final r except before a word beginning with a vowel, will omit it or pronounce it, in accordance with their own custom.

2. Practice Sentences for r Sound

Find the words in these sentences which contain the r sound.　Read the sentences aloud slowly and carefully.

1.　Robert has a pet rabbit.

2.　The rabbit ran away.

3.　Robert ran after the rabbit.

4.　The rabbit ran behind the rock.

5.　Round and round and round he ran.

6.　Robert called Roy to find a carrot.

7.　Roy put the carrot by the rock.

8.　The rabbit ran to get the carrot.

9.　Robert reached for the rabbit but he ran away.

3. Completion Game for r Sound

Find the right word to complete the sentence.

1.　A rabbit can
　　　　read　　　row　　　run

2.　A rabbit likes to eat
　　　　arrows　　　carrots　　　fairies

3.　Robert ran to catch the
　　　　river　　　rock　　　rabbit

Write some additional sentences which contain the r sound in your Work Book.　The word lists on the opposite page will help you.

4. br[1]

Say these words slowly. Listen for the r sound.

bring	bread	broom	umbrella
brick	breast	broke	redbreast
bridge	breath	break	gingerbread
brown	breakfast	brave	*abroad
brought	brush	branch	*library
bright	brother	brass	*celebrate

Find the br words in these sentences. Read the sentences aloud.

1. Please run to the store and bring some bread.
2. Daddy brought the bread last night.
3. May I have some bread and jam for breakfast?
4. Daddy did not remember to bring the jam.
5. Look at Robin Redbreast on that branch.
6. He brought a bug to his baby for breakfast.
7. May I give Robin Redbreast some bread?
8. Robert read in our reader about Robin Redbreast.
9. I read the story of "The Gingerbread Man."
10. The Gingerbread Man ran away.

Write some additional sentences in your Work Book using the above word lists.

---

* Not in Gates or Thorndike Primary Word Lists.   [1] See also page 20.

5. cr

Say these words slowly. Listen for the r sound.

			scr-[1]
cry	cradle	cream	scream
cried	crayon	creep	scrub
cross	crack	creature	scratch
crowd	cracker	crept	scramble
crown	crab	across	*describe
crib	crawl	scarecrow	

Find the cr words in these sentences. Read the sentences aloud.

1. Mary is crying and Bobby is crying.

2. Bobby is in his cradle.

3. He is crying for a cracker.

4. Mary is crying for an ice cream cone.

5. Mary has lost her crayon.

6. She had a big red crayon.

7. Her crayon box was across the room.

8. Someone took her red crayon.

9. Mary was very cross.

10. She ran to her mother and cried.

Write some additional sentences in your Work Book using the above word lists.

* Not in Gates or Thorndike Primary Word Lists.   [1] See also page 71.

6. <u>dr</u>

Say these words slowly.   Listen for the <u>r</u> sound.

draw	dry	drink	children
drew	dried	drank	hundred
dress	drive	*drunk	*snowdrift
drop	driver	*drag	*adrift
drum	drove	*drug	*withdraw
dream	drown	*drill	*cathedral

Find the <u>dr</u> words in these sentences.   Read the sentences aloud.

1.   You may draw a picture of your drum.

2.   Do not drop your drum.

3.   Is your dress dry?

4.   When your dress is dry you may go for a drive.

5.   The driver stopped to let the horses drink.

6.   Are the children dressed for the drive?

7.   The children have been dressed an hour.

8.   May we drive by the cathedral?

9.   The cathedral is over a hundred years old.

10.   May I draw a picture of the cathedral tomorrow?

Write some additional sentences in your Work Book using the above word lists.

_____

* Not in Gates or Thorndike Primary Word Lists.

7. fr[1]

Say these words slowly. Listen for the r sound.

friend	free	fright	Fred
from	freeze	frighten	Frank
frog	frozen	front	Frances
frolic	frost	*fried	Friday
fresh	frosty	*freedom	afraid
fruit	frisky	*frequent	Alfred

Find the fr words in these sentences. Read the sentences aloud.

1. My best friend is named Fred.
2. Fred came from Virginia.
3. We get fresh fruit from his farm.
4. Fred picks the fruit every Friday.
5. Fred thinks we may have frost tonight.
6. Last winter the fruit was frozen.
7. Fred's father is afraid the fruit will freeze again.
8. Fred and Frank caught a frog in front of the house.
9. I was afraid to touch the frog.
10. Do you like fried frog legs?

Write some additional sentences in your Work Book using the above word lists.

---

* Not in Gates or Thorndike Primary Word Lists.   [1] See also page 28.

8. gr[1]

Say these words slowly. Listen for the <u>r</u> sound.

grew	grass	ground	hungry
grow	grand	growl	agree
grown	grandma	grain	*degree
gray	grandpa	grade	*disgrace
great	green	grace	*paragraph
grape	greedy	gruff	*congratulate

Find the <u>gr</u> words in these sentences. Read the sentences aloud.

1. I went to visit grandma.
2. Grandma lives in a great big house.
3. Grandma is a grand old lady.
4. She has gray hair.
5. Grandpa has a great big dog named Rover.
6. I like to run on the green grass with Rover.
7. Grandma bought some grapes at the grocery store.
8. Rover growled and growled at the grocer boy.
9. I was hungry and ate all the grapes.
10. Grandma said, "Don't be greedy."

Write some additional sentences in your Work Book using the above word lists.

---

* Not in Gates or Thorndike Primary Word Lists.   [1] See also page 102.

9. <u>pr</u>

Say these words slowly. Listen for the <u>r</u> sound.

pray	prince	prefer	<u>spr-</u>[1]
praise	princess	prepare	spring
prayer	pretty	proper	sprinkle
practice	pride	April	spread
promise	prize	apron	sprang
present	proud	surprise	*sprung

Find the <u>pr</u> words in these sentences. Read the sentences aloud.

1. You may practice for the play.
2. The play is called, "The Prince and the Ruby Ring."
3. Robert may be the prince.
4. Rose may be the princess.
5. The prince wishes to marry the princess.
6. The princess is very pretty.
7. The prince brings a ruby ring to the princess.
8. He says, "I pray thee, pretty princess, wilt thou marry me?"
9. The princess promises to marry the prince.
10. The prince promises to protect the princess always.

Write some additional sentences in your Work Book using the above word lists.

---

* Not in Gates or Thorndike Primary Word Lists.   [1] See also page 77.

r DRILLS FOR SOUND OF R—continued

10. tr

Say these words slowly. Listen for the r sound.

try	train	trousers	str-[1]
tried	track	travel	street
tree	trick	trouble	stream
treat	truck	tremble	string
true	trunk	country	strong
truth	trust	*wintry	strange

Find the tr words in these sentences. Read the sentences aloud.

1. Please try to study your lesson.
2. I shall try to send my trunk today.
3. He tried to walk the train track.
4. My trunk is on the truck.
5. He took a trip to the country.
6. I told the truth about my trip.
7. May I trim the Christmas tree?
8. Look at the red berries on that tree!
9. The street car is near our street.
10. That strange man looks very strong.

Write some additional sentences in your Work Book using the above word lists.

* Not in Gates or Thorndike Primary Word Lists.   [1] See also page 79.

11. thr[1]

three	*thrush	*throb	*thrill
throw	*thrust	*throttle	*thrift
throat	*thrash	*throng	*thrifty
thread	*thresh	*threat	*thriftless
threw	*throne	*threaten	*overthrew
through	*throughout	*threatened	*overthrow

Find the thr words in these sentences. Read the sentences aloud.

1. I have three balls.
2. Three and three are six.
3. One, two, three, throw the ball to me.
4. Please throw the three balls to me.
5. He threw three balls to Robert.
6. My throat is not sore.
7. Have you three spools of thread?
8. I am through with those three spools of thread.
9. Mother has three needles but no thread.
10. The King sat on his throne throughout the service.

Write some additional sentences in your Work Book using the above word lists.

---

* Not in Gates or Thorndike Primary Word Lists.   [1] See also page 32:

12. shr[1]

Say these words slowly. Listen for the r sound.

*shrub	*shrink	*shred
*shrug	*shrank	*shrewd
*shriek	*shrunk	*shrine
*shrill	*shrivel	*shroud

Find the shr words in these sentences. Read the sentences aloud.

1. Here are the shrubs we planted.

2. These shrubs blossom in April.

3. Those shrubs grow very large.

4. One day my rabbit ran through the shrubs.

5. A dog was behind the largest shrub.

6. Ruth was so frightened, she shrieked.

7. She broke through the shrubbery.

8. Ruth's dress was torn to shreds.

9. The dog shrank away.

10. I heard Ruth when she shrieked.

Write some additional sentences in your Work Book using the above word lists.

---

* Not in Gates or Thorndike Primary Word Lists.   [1] See also page 86.

13. Completion Game for r Sound

Find the right word to complete the sentence.

1. Robin Redbreast sat on a
   drop   branch   bread   drink

2. The child cried for some ice-
   crayon   grass   cream   grain

3. The driver gave his horses a
   broom   train   drum   drink

4. It is so cold I am afraid the fruit will
   thread   freeze   throne   friend

5. In spring the grass is
   grace   proud   green   drop

6. The prince wished to marry the
   train   grape   prize   princess

7. Robin Redbreast comes in the
   string   stream   spring   scrap

Write some additional sentences in your Work Book. Use as many words containing the r sound as possible.

14. Poems Containing the r Sound[1]

You will enjoy the poems in Group 12, page 174. Choose a poem to learn and recite to the class.

---

[1] For use of poems, consult *Plan of the Book*, page XIV.

DRILLS FOR SOUND OF S

Webster: s
I.P.A.: [s]

1. Word Drill for s Sound

Say the following words slowly.   Listen for the s sound.

Initial	Initial	Medial	Medial
say	sat	pussy	kissing
see	sad	mousie	missing
saw	sand	pencil	guessing
so	sang	answer	dancing
same	set	myself	passing
seem	sell	herself	tossing
seen	send	himself	dressing
seed	sent	sunset	crossing
sea	cent	seesaw	chasing
seat	said	saucer	placing
side	sit	inside	yesterday
sign	sing	outside	Christmas
sigh	sink	beside	December
soap	silk	aside	message
sold	since	useful	messenger
suit	some	bicycle	policeman
soup	son	grocer	gasoline
soon	sun	grocery	necessary
sir	sunny	Lucy	possible
search	such	Bessie	Betsy

NOTE: The teacher should explain that *other spellings* represent the sound of s as in *see*, for example: cent, ice, box (bo*x*).

2. Practice Sentences for s Sound

Find the words in these sentences which contain the s sound. Read the sentences aloud slowly and carefully.

1. Did you hear Sue sing her new song?

2. I heard her sing her song yesterday.

3. Today Sue will sing a song about Santa.

4. Santa will soon be here.

5. Santa will bring Sam a sailor suit.

6. Lucy said she wanted a seesaw.

7. Bessie said she wanted a bicycle.

8. Sam will sing a song about a sailor boy.

9. The sailor went to sea.

3. Completion Game for s Sound

Find the right word to complete the sentence.

1. Sue sang a song about
   summer   Santa   sand

2. Sam sang a song about a
   Santa   Bessie   sailor

3. Santa will bring Lucy a
   yesterday   seesaw   dancing

Write some additional sentences which contain the s sound in your Work Book. The word lists on the opposite page will help you.

4. Word Drill for s Sound—continued

Say the following words slowly. Listen for the s sound.

Final	-fs (-ghs)	-ls	-ts
us	roofs	else	hats
ice	laughs	*false	rats
nice	**-ks (-x)**[1]	**-ns (-nce)**	kites
mice	books	once	nuts
mouse	looks	since	pets
house	likes	fence	goats
horse	makes	dance	paints
miss	cakes	**-ps**	**-sts**
kiss	rocks	caps	nests
this	ducks	cups	rests
geese	chicks	tops	guests
goose	drinks	hops	dusts
guess	ax	hopes	trusts
yes	fix	ropes	posts
bus	fox	keeps	wastes
pass	box	peeps	tastes
grass	ox	lips	costs
face	oxen	helps	**-ths**
place	six	jumps	months
piece	*sixty	bumps	lengths

---

* Not in Gates or Thorndike Primary Word Lists.   [1] See also page 104.

5. Completion Game for s Sound

Find the right word to complete the sentence.

1. Sam saw a girl sitting in the
       ice   mice   horse   house

2. Miss Bess saw a man sitting on a
       mice   mouse   horse   goose

3. Sue saw a bird sitting on a
       dance   fence   mice   since

4. A cat likes to eat
       miss   mice   nice   bus

5. A horse likes to eat
       books   goose   grass   chicks

6. We want some goats for
       hats   pets   paints   kites

7. Our cook bakes nice
       books   cooks   cakes   makes

8. When I go to the city, I ride on a
       bus   ice   house   mouse

Write some additional sentences in your Work Book. Use as many words containing the s sound as possible.

6. sc (sk)[1]

Say these words slowly.   Listen for the s sound.

sky	skirt	*scar	ask
skip	scold	*scarf	*task
skin	scale	*scholar	desk
skate	scare	*scold	*dusk
school	scamper	*score	asks
scooter	scarlet	*Scotch	desks

Find the sc (sk) words in these sentences.   Read the sentences aloud.

1. Look at the sky.

2. Can you skip?

3. Can you skate?

4. Do you like to skate to school?

5. I have a scooter but only one skate.

6. May I take my scooter to school?

7. Will you ask your mother if you may skate to school?

8. Daddy gave me a scooter and a pair of skates.

9. I have a fine desk at school.

10. I keep my lunch basket on my desk at school.

Write some additional sentences in your Work Book using the above word lists.

* Not in Gates or Thorndike Primary Word Lists.   [1] See also pages 96 and 98.

7. scr[1]

Say these words slowly. Listen for the s sound.

scream	*screen	*screw	describe
scrub	*screech	*scruple	description
scratch	*screak	*scroll	*subscribe
scrap	*scrape	*scrim	*subscriber
scramble	*scraper	*scripture	*subscription
*scribble	*scrawl	*scribe	*postscript

Find the scr words in these sentences. Read the sentences aloud.

1. Did the kitten scratch you?
2. When the kitten scratched me, I screamed.
3. Scrub, scrub, scrub your hands.
4. I haven't a scrap of paper.
5. Have you the screw for the screen?
6. Describe the screw you wish for the screen.
7. Did you scrub the screen?
8. Never scribble on your desk!
9. May I have some scrambled eggs?
10. The screech owl screeched and screamed all night.

Write some additional sentences in your Work Book using the above word lists.

---

* Not in Gates or Thorndike Primary Word Lists.   [1] See also page 57.

8. sl[1]

Say these words slowly.   Listen for the s sound.

slow	sleigh	*slate	*sleet
sleep	sly	*slave	*sleeve
sleepy	slide	*slim	*sleek
slept	slip	*sling	*slick
sled	slipper	*slang	asleep

Find the sl words in these sentences.   Read the sentences aloud.

1. Mother sang to the baby, "Sleep, baby, sleep."

2. The baby went to sleep at seven o'clock.

3. I am sleepy also.

4. Why do you sleep so much, Sleepy-head?

5. I slept soundly until seven o'clock this morning.

6. Mother slept so soundly we were late to school.

7. I slipped into her room at seven o'clock.

8. She was asleep.

9. The baby was asleep.

10. Our clock was slow, also.

Write some additional sentences in your Work Book using the above word lists.

---

* Not in Gates or Thorndike Primary Word Lists.   [1] See also page 51.

9. <u>sm</u>

Say these words slowly.   Listen for the <u>s</u> sound.

small	*smock	*smith	*smut
smell	*smack	*smithy	*smug
smile	*smash	*smoker	*smuggle
smoke	*smear	*smote	*smudge
smooth	*smelt	*smolder	*smother

Find the <u>sm</u> words in these sentences.   Read the sentences aloud.

1.   May I smell the flower?

2.   I smell smoke.

3.   Do you smell smoke?

4.   Please smile for me.

5.   That small child smiled at me.

6.   How much smaller are you than your brother?

7.   Daddy smokes a cigar every day.

8.   I did not smash my finger.

9.   Betty has smut on her new smock.

10.   The ice is very smooth on the pond.

    Write some additional sentences in your Work Book using the above word lists.

---

* Not in Gates or Thorndike Primary Word Lists.

10. <u>sn</u>

Say these words slowly. Listen for the <u>s</u> sound.

snow	*snap	*snail	*snatch
snowy	*snip	*snipe	*snort
snowball	*snub	*sneak	*snare
snowflake	*snug	*sneaker	*snarl
snake	*snuff	*sniff	*snoop
sneeze	*snob	*snicker	*sneer

Find the <u>sn</u> words in these sentences. Read the sentences aloud.

1. Look at the snow.
2. Can you make a snowball?
3. We made a snow man.
4. My puppies are named Snip and Snap.
5. Have you seen Snip and Snap?
6. Snip and Snap like to run in the snow.
7. Snap looks like a snowball.
8. We saw a snake near our house.
9. Snip was afraid of the snake.
10. Snap went very close to the snake.

Write some additional sentences in your Work Book using the above word lists.

---

* Not in Gates or Thorndike Primary Word Lists.

11. sp

Say these words slowly. Listen for the s sound.

spoon	spend	spark	*lisp
spin	spent	sparkle	*wisp
spill	spade	respect	*wasp
speak	spot	inspect	*gasp
spoke	spoil	*despise	*grasp
spider	sparrow	*despair	*clasp

Find the sp words in these sentences. Read the sentences aloud.

1. I have a spoon.
2. I have a spade.
3. May I have your spoon?
4. I left my spoon and spade in your yard.
5. Can you spin a top?
6. Did you spill the water?
7. Will you speak to me?
8. You should speak when you are spoken to.
9. Do you lisp?
10. When you make your speech, try not to lisp.

Write some additional sentences in your Work Book using the above word lists.

---

* Not in Gates or Thorndike Primary Word Lists.

12. spl[1]

Say these words slowly. Listen for the s sound.

splash	*split	*splotch
splashed	*splint	*splatter
splendid	*splinter	*splasher
*splendidly	*splintered	*splurge
*splendor	*splice	*splicer

Find the spl words in these sentences. Read the sentences aloud.

1. Do not splash me.

2. Splash! Splash! Splash! went the fish in the pond.

3. The baby splashed and splashed in her tub.

4. The goldfish splashed in the bowl.

5. That is a splendid piece of work.

6. I have a splinter in my finger.

7. He split the wood into splinters.

8. My arm is in a splint.

9. My dress is splattered with mud.

10. He spliced the ropes.

Write some additional sentences in your Work Book using the above word lists.

___
* Not in Gates or Thorndike Primary Word Lists.   [1] See also page 50.

13. spr[1]

Say these words slowly.   Listen for the s sound.

spring	*spray	*spry
sprinkle	*sprawl	*spree
spread	*sprig	*sprite
sprang	*spruce	*sprightly
sprung	*sprout	*sprain

Find the spr words in these sentences.   Read the sentences aloud.

1. Spring is here! Spring is here!

2. The robin will come in the spring.

3. Did you sprinkle the grass?

4. Our cat sprang to catch the mouse.

5. Our dog sprang up with joy.

6. Mother will spread butter on your bread.

7. I like to see a bird spread its wings.

8. Did you sprain your foot?

9. Every spring the buds begin to sprout.

10. Fairies spread green sprouts on every sprig.

Write some additional sentences in your Work Book using the above word lists.

---

* Not in Gates or Thorndike Primary Word Lists.   [1] See also page 61.

14. st

Say these words slowly. Listen for the s sound.

star	stay	upstairs	east
start	stand	downstairs	west
stop	stamp	understand	nest
store	step	understood	best
story	stair	door-step	must
stove	still	haystack	lost

Find the st words in these sentences. Read the sentences aloud.

1. We have a toy store.
2. Sam made a stamp book for the store.
3. Sarah brought some stick candy to put in the store.
4. I brought a little toy stove.
5. We have a beautiful story book in the store.
6. The best story is called "Jack and the Beanstalk."
7. Jack tried to climb the beanstalk.
8. Sue made a lovely gold star to hang in the store.
9. She called it "The Star in the East."
10. Do you know the story of "The Star in the East?"

Write some additional sentences in your Work Book using the above word lists.

15. str[1]

Say these words slowly. Listen for the s sound.

street	straw	struggle	*destroy
stream	strip	stretch	*instruct
string	stripe	strength	*construct
strong	strike	*stranger	*obstruct
strange	stroke	*strain	*restrict
straight	struck	*strainer	*restrain

Find the str words in these sentences. Read the sentences aloud.

1. I live on Cedar Street.
2. There is a stream near our street.
3. We sail a sail-boat on the stream.
4. We tie the boat to a stick with a string.
5. One day the string broke.
6. The sail-boat sailed down the stream.
7. It sailed straight to the bank.
8. Jack had a hard struggle to reach it.
9. He stretched out his arm and caught the boat.
10. After that, we bought a stronger piece of string.

Write some additional sentences in your Work Book using the above word lists.

---

* Not in Gates or Thorndike Primary Word Lists.   [1] See also page 62.

16. sw

Say these words slowly. Listen for the s sound.

sweet	sweater	swan	*swear
sweep	swept	swallow	*swore
swim	swift	*swiftly	*sworn
swimming	swimmer	*sweetly	*switch
swing	swam	*sweeten	*Swiss
swinging	swum	*swell	*Sweden

Find the sw words in these sentences. Read the sentences aloud.

1. Bessie and I went swimming today.
2. Bessie swam across the lake.
3. We swam a long time.
4. I wore my sweater after I came from swimming.
5. Bessie wore her sweater also.
6. After we went swimming, we sat in the swing.
7. Then I swept the floor.
8. I often sweep the floor for Mother.
9. Did you see the swan today?
10. The swan swam swiftly away.

Write some additional sentences in your Work Book using the above word lists.

---

* Not in Gates or Thorndike Primary Word Lists.

17. squ(skw)[1]

Say these words slowly.   Listen for the s sound.

square	*squaw	*squash
squeak	*squall	*squashy
squeaky	*squawk	*squander
squeal	*squat	*squirm
squeeze	*squatty	*squire
squirrel	*squelch	*squalor

Find the squ words in these sentences.   Read the sentences aloud.

1. We sat in the square.
2. The baby saw a squirrel.
3. The squirrel ran around the square.
4. The baby squealed and squealed.
5. I want to hold the squirrel.
6. Do not squeeze the tiny squirrel.
7. We heard a saw go squeak, squeak, squeak.
8. We saw a squaw squatting in the sun.
9. The squaw had a bowl of squash.
10. The squirrel sat near the squaw.

Write some additional sentences in your Work Book using the above word lists.

---

* Not in Gates or Thorndike Primary Word Lists.   [1] See also page 100.

z

DRILLS FOR SOUND OF S (Z)

I.P.A.: [z]

18. Word Drill for z (voiced s) Sound[1]

Say the following words slowly.   Listen for the z sound.

Initial	Final	-bz	-nz
*zoo	is	webs	pans
*zebra	his	tubs	pens
*zeal	as	robs	hens
*zone	has	**-dz**	horns
*zinc	was	adds	rains
*zest	does	reads	signs
*Zion	goes	heads	opens
Medial	nose	**-gz**	**-ngz**
easy	rose	eggs	songs
busy	eyes	pigs	sings
lazy	wise	dogs	rings
daisy	rise	**-lz**	**-thz**
pansy	bees	dolls	clothes
visit	buzz	tells	truths
buzzing	ours	girls	smooths
husband	those	**-mz**	**-vz**
present	these	homes	gives
Thursday	cheese	seems	leaves
music	choose	rooms	loves
scissors	always	drums	moves

* Not in Gates or Thorndike Primary Word Lists.
[1] The teacher should explain that the z sound (z as in zoo) may be represented by the letter s; for example: is (iz), has (haz).

DRILLS FOR SOUND OF S (Z)—continued **Z**

19. Practice Sentences for z (voiced s) Sound

Find the words in these sentences which contain the z sound. Read the sentences aloud slowly and carefully.

1. Rose lives near the zoo.

2. The zebra lives in the zoo.

3. Rose goes to see the zebra often.

4. She goes to see the bears.

5. She visits the lions and the tigers.

6. Rose's brother loves animals.

7. He has two dogs.

8. He reads many stories about dogs.

9. He tells the stories to Rose.

20. Completion Game for z (voiced s) Sound

Read the beginning of the sentence. Find the word in the group which completes the sentence correctly.

1. The zebra's home is in the
    zinc   zoo   zone   zion

2. When Rose visits the zoo she sees
    dolls   drums   bears   rains

3. Rose's brother has two
    bugs   pigs   dogs   webs

Write some additional sentences which contain the z sound in your Work Book. The word lists on the opposite page will help you.

21. Review Sentences for s and z Sounds

1. Lucy and Bessie are sisters.

2. Their cousin's name is Sue.

3. Sue lives in a white house.

4. Lucy and Bessie went to visit their cousin.

5. Bessie stayed all summer.

6. Lucy was homesick and would not stay.

7. Bessie and Sue went swimming.

8. Sue is a better swimmer than Bessie.

9. Bessie splashes the water when she dives.

10. Bessie went home in September.

11. School begins in September.

12. Lucy and Bessie started to school.

13. Lucy likes school.

14. She likes to study her speech lesson.

15. She is studying music.

22. Completion Game for s and z Sounds

Find the right word to complete the sentence.

1. Santa brought Sam a sailor
    soap   salt   suit   sing

2. I saw Sam riding on a
    house   horse   cross   mice

3. Sue has a fine desk at
    skate   stool   school   stay

4. Sue went to bed early because she was
    slipper   sleepy   slowly   slide

5. When it snows, we make a
    smoke man   snow man   snap man

6. Flowers bloom in the
    string   spring   sprang   strange

7. Last night I looked at the sky and saw
    some stars   some steps   some skates

Write some additional sentences in your Work Book. Use as many words containing the s and z sounds as possible.

23. Poems Containing the s and z Sounds[1]

You will enjoy the poems in Group 13, page 177. Choose a poem to learn and recite to the class.

---

[1] For use of poems, consult *Plan of the Book*, page XIV.

sh

Webster: sh
I.P.A.: [ʃ]

1. Word Drill for sh Sound

Say the following words slowly.   Listen for the sh sound.

Initial	Initial	Medial	Final
she	shed	washes	wash
sheep	shelf	wishes	wish
sheet	shell	dishes	dish
shall	shout	fishes	fish
should	shower	radishes	radish
shoe	shore	pushes	push
show	shoulder	bushes	bush
shut	sharp	brushes	brush
ship	shoot	brushing	hush
shop	short	rushes	rush
shot	**shr-**[1]	crushes	crush
shock	*shrank	dashes	dash
shine	*shrink	splashes	splash
shone	*shrimp	finishes	finish
shook	*shrill	sunshine	fresh
shake	*shriek	seashore	flesh
shade	*shred	ashamed	flash
shape	*shrug	ocean	trash
shame	*shrub	nation	English
shirt	*shrew	station	foolish

---

* Not in Gates or Thorndike Primary Word Lists.   [1] See also page 64.

NOTE: The teacher should explain that various *other spellings* represent the sound of *sh* as in *she*, for example: *ocean, nation, machine, sugar, delicious, Chicago, conscious.*

2. Practice Sentences for sh Sound

Find the words in these sentences which contain the sh sound.   Read the sentences aloud slowly and carefully.

1.   Shirley and I made a toy shop.

2.   Shall I show you the toys in our shop?

3.   Here is the ship Marcia gave us.

4.   Marcia bought the ship at the seashore.

5.   She found those shells by the ocean.

6.   Shirley brought the toy fishes and fisherman.

7.   She gave us the sheep and the shepherd.

8.   Shirley's mother gave us a little dish.

9.   Shirley's father gave us a tiny fish.

3. Completion Game for sh Sound

Read the beginning of the sentence.   Find the word in the group which completes the sentence correctly.

1.   In the toy shop we saw a
shake   ship   shape

2.   Shirley brought some
brushes   fishes   wishes

3.   Shirley's mother gave her a
push   brush   dish

Write some additional sentences which contain the sh sound in your Work Book.   The word lists on the opposite page will help you.

4. zh (sh voiced)[1]

Say these words slowly.   Listen for the zh sound.

usual	*vision	*confusion	*leisure
measure	*division	*conclusion	*seizure
pleasure	*decision	*collision	*azure
treasure	*persuasion	*invasion	*rouge
occasion	*explosion	*delusion	*garage

Find the zh words in these sentences.   Read the sentences aloud.

1. She came late as usual.

2. Shall I measure this?

3. She will come with pleasure.

4. Please show me your treasures.

5. I accept the treasure with pleasure.

6. She showed me an example in long division.

7. Shall I drive the car to the garage?

8. It is a pleasure to welcome you on this occasion.

9. After much persuasion he showed us his treasures.

10. The collision caused the explosion.

Write some additional sentences in your Work Book using the above word lists.

---

* Not in Gates or Thorndike Primary Word Lists.

[1] The teacher should explain that various *other spellings* represent the *zh* sound, for example: vision, measure, usual, rou*ge*.

5. Review Sentences for sh and zh Sounds

Find the words in these sentences which contain the sh and zh sounds. Read the sentences aloud slowly and carefully.

1. Are you sure you wish to see our show?

2. I shall accept your invitation with pleasure.

3. Bob wishes to be the fisherman, as usual.

4. He dashes in shrieking, "Ship Ahoy! Ship Ahoy!"

5. He rushes and rushes around.

6. I wish that he would not shout so.

7. The fisherman lives near the ocean.

6. Completion Game for sh and zh Sounds

Read the beginning of the sentence. Find the word in the group which completes the sentence correctly.

1. You may have your shoes shined at a

   toy shop   shoe shop   pet shop

2. After dinner mother washes the

   fishes   sunshine   dishes

3. Do you wish me to show you our

   leisure?   pleasure?   treasure?

Write some additional sentences which contain the sh and zh sounds in your Work Book. Use as many words containing these sounds as possible.

7. Poems Containing the sh and zh Sounds[1]

You will enjoy the poems in Group 14, page 186. Choose a poem to learn and recite to the class.

---

[1] For use of poems, consult *Plan of the Book*, page XIV.

ch

DRILLS FOR SOUND OF Ch

Webster: ch
I.P.A.: [tʃ]

1. Word Drill for ch Sound

Say the following words slowly. Listen for the ch sound.

Initial	Medial	Final
chair	teacher	each
child	teaches	teach
chick	reaches	reach
chicken	peaches	peach
chipmunk	speeches	speech
children	kitchen	much
chin	butcher	such
chalk	pitcher	which
check	riches	rich
cheese	witches	witch
choose	watches	watch
chose	marches	march
cherry	churches	church
chase	searches	search
change	branches	branch
chain	catches	catch
chap	hatches	hatch
chapter	matches	match
chop	touches	touch

2. Practice Sentences for <u>ch</u> Sound

Find the words in these sentences which contain the <u>ch</u> sound.   Read the sentences aloud slowly and carefully.

1.   May I choose the children for our play?

2.   Charles may be Charlie Chipmunk.

3.   Richard may be Little Chick.

4.   I choose to be an Indian Chief.

5.   One child may be a Dutch boy.

6.   The Indian Chief will make a speech.

7.   The Dutch boy must catch Little Chick.

3. Completion Game for <u>ch</u> Sound

Read the beginning of the sentence.   Find the word in the group which completes the sentence correctly.

1.   All the children marched to their

    chews   cheese   chairs   chains

2.   The boy chosen for Little Chick was named

    kitchen   Charlie   riches   Richard

3.   A speech was made by an

    Indian child   Indian Chief   Charles

Write some additional sentences which contain the <u>ch</u> sound in your Work Book.   The word lists on the opposite page will help you.

4. Poems Containing the <u>ch</u> Sound[1]

You will enjoy the poems in Group 15, page 189.   Choose a poem to learn and recite to the class.

---

[1] For use of poems, consult *Plan of the Book*, page XIV.

j

DRILLS FOR SOUND OF J

Webster: j
I.P.A.: [dʒ]

1. Word Drill for j Sound

Say the following words slowly.   Listen for the j sound.

Initial	Medial	Final
jar	pigeon	age
jaw	engine	cage
joy	pages	page
join	larger	large
jump	largest	charge
just	gingerbread	change
joke	vegetable	strange
jerk	danger	village
jelly	dangerous	cabbage
jacket	angel	message
Jack	bridges	bridge
James	soldier	porridge
John	enjoy	orange
January	rejoice	carriage
June	reject	cottage
July	object	college
gee	magic	language
giant	tragic	urge
gentle	*suggest	edge
general	*injure	judge

* Not in Gates or Thorndike Primary Word Lists.

NOTE: The teacher should explain that various *other spellings* represent the sound of *j* as in *jar*, for example: en*g*ine, bri*dg*e, sol*d*ier.

2. Practice Sentences for j Sound

Find the words in these sentences which contain the j sound. Read the sentences aloud slowly and carefully.

1. John played a joke on James.

2. John had a jumping-jack in a large box.

3. John said, "Here is a magic box, James."

4. James jerked open the strange box.

5. Out jumped a large jumping-jack.

6. James jumped as high as the jumping-jack.

7. James said, "I enjoyed that joke."

3. Completion Game for j Sound

Read the beginning of the sentence. Find the word in the group which completes the sentence correctly.

1. James did not know John was playing a

      jump   jerk   joke   June

2. John played a joke with a

      gingerbread   jumping-jack   vegetable

3. John told James he had a

      charge box   orange box   magic box

Write some additional sentences which contain the j sound in your Work Book. The word lists on the opposite page will help you.

4. Poems Containing the j Sound[1]

You will enjoy the poems in Group 16, page 192. Choose a poem to learn and recite to the class.

---

[1] For use of poems, consult *Plan of the Book*, page XIV.

y DRILLS FOR SOUND OF Y

Webster: y
I.P.A.: [j]

1. Word Drills for y Sound

Say the following words slowly. Listen for the y sound.

Initial	Initial	Medial
you	*ye	barnyard
your	*yield	beyond
year	*yeast	onion
yet	*yacht	opinion
yes	*yawn	companion
yesterday	*yarn	union
yellow	*yearn	million
yard	*yon	William
young	*yonder	Daniel
younger	*yolk	Italian
youngest	*youngster	*junior
youth	*youthful	*senior
you'll	*yea	*lawyer
you're	*yew	*canyon
you've	*yeoman	*familiar
you'd	*yore	*peculiar
yours	*York	*civilian

* Not in Gates or Thorndike Primary Word Lists.

2. Practice Sentences for y Sound

Find the words in these sentences which contain the y sound.   Read the sentences aloud slowly and carefully.

1. Would you like to wear your yellow dress?

2. Yes, if you do not care.

3. Are you going to play in your yard?

4. You must not go beyond the gate.

5. Yesterday Daniel went to the barnyard.

6. What is the name of your youngest brother?

7. My youngest brother is named William.

3. Completion Game for y Sound

Read the beginning of the sentence.   Find the word in the group which completes the sentence correctly.

1. My new dress is the color of yours.   It is
     younger   yet   yellow   years

2. Do you keep your horses in a
     barnyard?   onion?   opinion?   beyond?

3. Your little brother must be almost six
     yards old   years old   yachts old

Write some additional sentences which contain the y sound in your Work Book.   The word lists on the opposite page will help you.

4. Poems Containing the y Sound[1]

You will enjoy the poems in Group 17, page 194.   Choose a poem to learn and recite to the class.

---

[1] For use of poems, consult *Plan of the Book*, page XIV.

k

DRILLS FOR SOUND OF K

Webster: k
I.P.A.: [k]

1. Word Drill for k Sound

Say the following words slowly.   Listen for the k sound.

Initial	Initial	cl-	Medial
car	key	clay	monkey
cow	keep	climb	donkey
came	kept	close	turkey
come	kite	cloud	pumpkin
can	king	clown	bucket
can't	kiss	**cr-**	jacket
cat	kitten	cry	pocket
cap	kitty	cried	because
cup	kill	cream	become
cut	kid	crown	became
coat	could	crowd	buttercup
cold	card	**sk- (sc-)**	cracker
coal	cart	sky	cooky
count	color	skate	pancake
call	cover	skin	picnic
corn	care	scare	picture
caught	carry	**scr-**	circus
cough	carrot	scream	stocking
cage	cool	scratch	basket
cake	curl	scrub	across

NOTE: The teacher should explain that the k sound (k as in key) may be represented by the letter c, for example: cup (kup), call (kall).

DRILLS FOR SOUND OF K—continued **k**

2. Practice Sentences for k Sound

Find the words in these sentences which contain the k sound.   Read the sentences aloud slowly and carefully.

1.   Carl came in the car today.

2.   It was so cold that he wore a coat to keep warm.

3.   Kate could not come because she had a cough.

4.   Carl came to see the mother cat and baby kittens.

5.   Kate is Carl's sister.

6.   Carl will carry a kitten to Kate.

7.   He will carry the kitten home in a basket.

8.   Carl will be careful not to hurt the kitten.

9.   Carl will give the kitten some breakfast.

3. Completion Game for k Sound

Read the beginning of the sentence.   Find the word in the group which completes the sentence correctly.

1.   Carl saw some baby kittens and a mother
   cow calf cat coat

2.   Carl carried a kitten home in a
   buttercup bucket basket

3.   The kitten will have milk for
   picnic breakfast pumpkin

Write some additional sentences which contain the k sound in your Work Book.   The word lists on the opposite page will help you.

k DRILLS FOR SOUND OF K—continued

4. Word Drill for k Sound

Say the following words slowly. Listen for the k sound.

Final	Final	-sk[1]	-sks
book	cake	ask	asks
look	cook	desk	desks
like	cock	task	tasks
lake	clock	mask	masks
wake	cluck	tusk	tusks
bake	crack	**-ks (-x)[2]**	**-ct (-ked)**
rake	take	books	baked
rock	took	cooks	cooked
sock	tick	looks	looked
lock	tock	likes	liked
block	stick	wakes	waked
back	walk	walks	walked
oak	talk	talks	talked
duck	milk	milks	milked
sick	thank	thanks	thanked
pick	think	thinks	barked
work	ink	six	parked
bark	pink	ox	marked
park	sink	box	act
dark	drink	fox	fact

[1] See also page 70.   [2] See also pages 68 and 104.

5. Practice Sentences for k Sound

Find the words in these sentences which contain the <u>k</u> sound. Read the sentences aloud slowly and carefully.

1. Jack has a new book.

2. The book is called "White Duck and Black Chick."

3. White Duck and Black Chick took a walk in the park.

4. They heard someone call, "Come, Duck, Duck, Ducky."

5. They heard someone call, "Come, Chick, Chick, Chicky."

6. Black Chick said, "Is that King Fox?"

7. White Duck said, "I think King Fox is behind the rock."

8. Black Chick took one look at the rock.

9. It was not King Fox, but old Turkey Lurkey.

6. Completion Game for <u>k</u> Sound

Read the beginning of the sentence. Find the word in the group which completes the sentence correctly.

1. Jack had a book about a
    duck   pick   fork   lock

2. White Duck went for a walk with
    King Fox   Jack   Black Chick

3. White Duck heard someone call. It was
    Black Chick   Jack's book   Turkey Lurkey

Write some additional sentences which contain the <u>k</u> sound in your Work Book. The word lists on the opposite page will help you.

7. qu (kw)[1]

Say these words slowly. Listen for the qu(kw) sound.

			squ(skw-)[1]
quack	question	equal	
quick	quart	frequent	square
quite	quarter	require	squeak
quiet	quarrel	*request	squeal
queen	quantity	*banquet	squeeze
queer	quality	*earthquake	squirrel

Find the qu words in these sentences. Read the sentences aloud.

1. The cat went to see the queen.

2. Our teacher said, "Keep very quiet."

3. Are you quite sure you were quiet?

4. Bring a quarter for your milk.

5. How many quarts of milk will a quarter buy?

6. Come quietly and quickly to look at the ducks.

7. Mother Duck says, "Quack! Quack! Quack!"

8. The car wheel says, "Squeak! Squeak! Squeak!"

9. Come, look at the squirrel!

10. The baby squealed when she saw the squirrel.

Write some additional sentences in your Work Book using the above word lists.

---

* Not in Gates or Thorndike Primary Word Lists.   [1] See also page 81.

8. Review Sentences for k Sound

Find the words in these sentences which contain the k sound. Read the sentences aloud slowly and carefully.

1. Carl has a scooter and Jack has a kite.

2. Carl and Jack are Kate's brothers.

3. The car takes them to school.

4. They pay a quarter for milk to drink.

5. Kate has a little black kitten.

6. The kitten likes to drink milk.

7. Jack has a black squirrel.

8. He keeps the squirrel in a cage.

9. Completion Game for k Sound

Read the beginning of the sentence. Find the word in the group which completes the sentence correctly.

1. Jack and Kate go to school
   in a cup   in a car   in a can

2. The little kitten belongs to
   cook   Kate   Carl   Jack

3. The squirrel belongs to
   Carl   Charles   Kate   Jack

Write some additional sentences which contain the k sound in your Work Book. Use as many words containing this sound as possible.

10. Poems Containing the k Sound[1]

You will enjoy the poems in Group 18, page 196. Choose a poem to learn and recite to the class.

---

[1] For use of poems, consult *Plan of the Book*, page XIV.

DRILLS FOR SOUND OF G

1. Word Drill for g Sound

Say the following words slowly.   Listen for the g sound.

Initial	gl-[1]	Medial	Final
go	glad	begin	egg
goes	glass	began	leg
goat	glove	begun	beg
gold	glee	again	big
got	glory	ago	dig
get	*glow	piggy	pig
gate	*globe	bigger	dog
gave	*glade	biggest	log
game	*glare	wagon	hog
gay	**gr-[2]**	forget	frog
gain	grow	forgot	bug
give	grew	forgive	dug
girl	grass	forgave	hug
good	ground	together	rug
goose	gray	tiger	tug
geese	great	sugar	tag
guess	grape	August	bag
gun	grade	agree	wag
gone	grain	angry	rag
garden	green	hungry	flag

* Not in Gates or Thorndike Primary Word Lists.
[1] See also page 49.   [2] See also page 60.

2. Practice Sentences for g Sound

Find the words in these sentences which contain the g sound. Read the sentences aloud slowly and carefully.

1. "Good morning, little girl, where are you going?"

2. "I am going to dig in my garden."

3. The little girl opened the garden gate.

4. A big, fat pig ran through the garden gate.

5. "Get out of the garden, big, fat pig," said the girl.

6. "Go, Piggy, go! Get out of my garden," she said.

7. The big, fat pig said, "Good-bye, I will go."

3. Completion Game for g Sound

Read the beginning of the sentence. Find the word in the group which completes the sentence correctly.

1. A little girl went to dig
   in a game   in a wagon   in a garden

2. She saw a big, fat pig run through the
   goat   glass   gold   gate

3. The little girl said to the pig:
   "No, bigger."   "Do, Doggy."   "Go, Piggy."

Write some additional sentences which contain the g sound in your Work Book. The word lists on the opposite page will help you.

4. Poems Containing the g Sound[1]

You will enjoy the poems in Group 19, page 198. Choose a poem to learn and recite to the class.

---

[1] For use of poems, consult *Plan of the Book*, page XIV.

DRILLS FOR SOUND OF X

1. Word Drill for x(ks) Sound[1]

Say the following words slowly.   Listen for the ks sound.

-ks		-x (-ks)	
books	ax	axes	exercise
cooks	ox	oxen	excellent
looks	box	boxes	excite
likes	fox	foxes	except
ducks	fix	sixteen	expect
milks	six	sixty-six	explain

Find the words in these sentences which contain the x(ks) sound.   Read sentences aloud slowly and carefully.

1.   I am six years old.

2.   My brother's name is Max.

3.   He bought six new books.

4.   One of the books is about a red fox.

5.   Red Fox has six baby foxes.

6.   The little foxes live next door to some ducks.

7.   The ducks live in a box.

8.   The ducks are afraid of Red Fox.

Write some additional sentences in your Work Book using the above word lists.

[1] NOTE: The teacher should explain that *x* may represent the sound of *ks* as in box (bo*ks*), or the sound of *gz* as in exist (eg-*z*ist). See page 105. For additional drill for *ks* sound, see pages 68 and 98.

2. Word Drill for x(gz) Sound[1]

Say the following words.   Listen for the <u>gz</u> sound

	<u>-gz</u>			-<u>x</u>(-<u>gz</u>)
eggs	pigs	wags		exact
legs	digs	tags		exactly
logs	wigs	flags		example
dogs	bugs	bags		*examination
hogs	rugs	rags		*exaggerate
frogs	hugs	drags		*exasperate

Find the words in these sentences which contain the <u>x(gz)</u> sound.   Read the sentences aloud slowly and carefully.

1. I worked every example.

2. The first example was about eggs.

3. The second example was about pigs.

4. The third example was about flags.

5. Did you pass your examination?

6. I finished my examination at exactly ten o'clock.

7. The teacher was exasperated with the boys.

8. They did not finish their examination.

Write some additional sentences in your Work Book using the above word lists.

---

* Not in Gates or Thorndike Primary Word Lists.
[1] See footnote page 104.

ng

DRILLS FOR SOUND OF ng

Webster: ng
I.P.A.: [ŋ]

1. Word Drill for ng Sound

Say the following words slowly. Listen for the ng sound.

-ng	-ng	-nk (-ngk)
sing	coming	ink
sang	going	sink
song	nothing	pink
long	something	bank
ring	morning	thank
wing	evening	think
ding	running	thinks
king	walking	drinks
thing	dancing	monkey
young	singing	donkey
hung	swinging	**-ng (-ngg)**
hang	springing	finger
rang	ringing	longer
clang	dinging	longest
swing	banging	stronger
bring	clanging	strongest
spring	length	younger
string	strength	youngest
strong	lengthen	anger
among	strengthen	angry

2. Practice Sentences for ng Sound

Find the words in these sentences which contain the ng sound. Read the sentences aloud slowly and carefully.

1. Can you sing?

2. The bird sang a spring song

3. He sang, "Spring is coming! Spring is coming!"

4. Every evening I swing in my swing.

5. My brother and I sing songs until the bell rings.

6. The bell rings Ding! Dong! Ding! Dong! Ding!

7. We think it is fun to swing and sing.

3. Completion Game for ng Sound

Read the beginning of the sentence. Find the word in the group which completes the sentence correctly.

1. A bird sang a

    swing   sing   song

2. I like to

    swing   string   strong

3. When a bell rings it says

    king   wing   ding

Write some additional sentences which contain the ng sound in your Work Book. The word lists on the opposite page will help you.

4. Poems Containing the ng Sound[1]

You will enjoy the poems in Group 20, page 200. Choose a poem to learn and recite to the class.

---

[1] For use of poems, consult *Plan of the Book*, page XIV.

h

DRILLS FOR SOUND OF H

Webster: h
I.P.A.: [h]

1. Word Drill for h Sound

Say the following words slowly. Listen for the h sound.

Initial	Initial	Medial
he	him	behind
her	his	perhaps
how	hit	unhappy
house	hid	household
hat	hill	*behold
had	hair	*beheld
has	here	*behave
have	home	*behalf
hand	hole	*ahead
hang	hold	*overhead
hen	hose	*overhang
hay	hut	*somehow
hate	hush	*unholy
head	hug	*upheld
heard	hung	*uphold
hurt	hunt	*rehearse
hog	hope	*overhear
hop	whole	*inhabit
hot	who	*inherit
horse	whom	*Idaho

* Not in Gates or Thorndike Primary Word Lists.

2. Practice Sentences for h Sound

Find the words in these sentences which contain the h sound. Read the sentences aloud slowly and carefully.

1. How did you hurt your hand, Helen?

2. Henry hit it with a hammer.

3. He was making a hen house.

4. He asked me to help him.

5. He said, "Hold your hand up here."

6. The hammer slipped from his hand.

7. He was very unhappy about hurting me.

3. Completion Game for h Sound

Read the beginning of the sentence. Find the word in the group which completes the sentence correctly.

1. Henry hit Helen's hand with a
   hen   hammer   house

2. Henry was building a
   hat   horse   house

3. Helen was holding up her
   head   hand   hat

Write some additional sentences which contain the h sound in your Work Book. The word lists on the opposite page will help you.

4. Poems Containing the h Sound[1]

You will enjoy the poems in Group 21, page 201. Choose a poem to learn and recite to the class.

---

[1] For use of poems, consult *Plan of the Book*, page XIV.

PRACTICE EXERCISES

III. For the Vowels

e

Webster: ē
I.P.A.: [i]

1. Words Containing the Sound of e as in he

Say these words slowly.   Listen for the sound of e as in he.

he	key	eat	each
me	keep	seat	pea
we	peep	wheat	peach
see	sheep	meat	tea
seed	sleep	beat	teach
tree	feet	read	reach

Read the following sentences aloud, slowly and carefully.   Find the words containing the sound of e as in he.

1. Have you seen our peach tree?

2. We have a peach tree in our garden.

3. We have a seat under the tree.

4. We like to eat peaches.

5. Peter took three peaches to his teacher.

6. "These three peaches are for you," he said.

7. Peter's teacher thanked him for the peaches.

8. She read the story of "The Green Peach Tree."

Write some additional sentences in your Work Book using the above word lists.

NOTE: The teacher should explain that various *other spellings* represent the sound of *e* as in *he*, for example: *feet. peach, key, field, receive.*

Webster: ĭ
I.P.A.: [ɪ]

i

2. Words Containing the Sound of <u>i</u> as in <u>it</u>

Say these words slowly. Listen for the sound of <u>i</u> as in <u>it</u>.

is	did	big	kitty
his	hid	pig	city
him	hill	pink	pretty
hit	will	think	hilly
sit	fill	ring	Billy
give	till	king	Biddy

Read the following sentences aloud, slowly and carefully. Find the words containing the sound of <u>i</u> as in <u>it</u>.

1. The big white dog lives with Billy.

2. The little white kitten lives with Sally.

3. Sally gives the kitten milk to drink.

4. The little kitten is very pretty.

5. The big white dog plays with the little kitten.

6. He will not hurt the little kitten.

7. Sally has a little chicken.

8. The little chicken is named Biddy.

Write some additional sentences in your Work Book using the above word lists.

NOTE: The teacher should explain that various *other spellings* represent the sound of *i* as in *it*, for example: b**u**ild, b**u**sy, pret**t**y, h**y**mn, fat**t**y.

e

Webster: ĕ
I.P.A.: [ɛ]

3. Words Containing the Sound of e as in end.

Say these words slowly.   Listen for the sound of e as in end.

men	met	egg	head
hen	get	leg	bread
pen	pet	bed	said
ten	let	fed	says
tent	best	fell	any
sent	nest	tell	many

Read the following sentences aloud, slowly and carefully.   Find the words containing the sound of e as in end.

1. Ben has a little red hen.

2. Ben's uncle sent him the hen for a pet.

3. Ben keeps the hen in a pen.

4. He made the hen a nest.

5. The little red hen laid an egg.

6. Ben said, "I will get the egg."

7. "Let me get it," said Ted.

8. Ted is Ben's brother.

Write some additional sentences in your Work Book using the above word lists.

Note: The teacher should explain that various *other spellings* represent the sound of *e* as in *end*, for example: any, many, said, says, bread, friend.

DRILLS FOR VOWEL SOUNDS

a

4. Words Containing the Sound of <u>a</u> as in <u>care</u>

Say these words slowly.   Listen for the sound of <u>a</u> as in <u>care</u>.

rare	bear	hair	scare
fare	pear	pair	scarce
bare	wear	chair	prepare
dare	where	fair	compare
share	there	fairy	declare
spare	their	stair	stare

Read the following sentences aloud, slowly and carefully.   Find the words containing the sound of <u>a</u> as in <u>care</u>.

1. May we play "The Story of the Three Bears?"

2. Where are the chairs for the bears?

3. Here is Mother Bear's chair.

4. There is Baby Bear's chair.

5. Father Bear's chair is upstairs.

6. Betty has golden hair.   She may be Goldilocks.

7. Father Bear has gone upstairs to get his chair.

8. Mother Bear must take care of Baby Bear.

Write some additional sentences in your Work Book using the above word lists.

NOTE: The teacher should explain that various *other spellings* represent the sound of *a* as in *care*, for example: p*ear*, *air*, th*ere*, th*eir*.

5. Words Containing the Sound of a as in at

Say these words slowly.   Listen for the sound of a as in at.

hat	an	add	and
cat	can	bad	hand
sat	man	dad	sand
rat	ran	had	land
fat	rang	has	lamp
that	sang	have	stamp

Read the following sentences aloud, slowly and carefully.   Find the words containing the sound of a as in at.

1. Dan has a story called "The Two Black Cats."

2. Dan may stand and read the story of the black cats.

3. The two black cats had two little kittens.

4. The kittens were named Blacky and Tacky.

5. Blacky was fat with shiny black fur.

6. Tacky was thin with black and yellow fur.

7. Tacky can never, never catch a rat.

8. He always takes a nap in my lap.

Write some additional sentences in your Work Book using the above word lists.

DRILLS FOR VOWEL SOUNDS **a**

6. Words Containing the Sound of a as in ask[1]

Say these words slowly. Listen for the sound of a as in ask.

grass	last	dance	basket
glass	fast	chance	master
class	past	grant	after
pass	calf	plant	answer
path	half	aunt	rather
bath	laugh	can't	example

Read the following sentences aloud, slowly and carefully. Find the words containing the sound of a as in ask.

1. Our speech class meets at half-past nine.

2. The last speech class meets at half-past eleven.

3. I'd rather be in the last class.

4. My aunt took me to a dancing class last week.

5. Afterwards she gave me a basket full of plants.

6. We planted them by the path in our garden.

7. Mother planted many beautiful plants last summer.

8. Last winter, the frost killed every plant.

Write some additional sentences in your Work Book using the above word lists.

[1] See footnote page 134.

7. Words Containing the Sound of u̲ as in u̲p

Say these words slowly. Listen for the sound of u̲ as in u̲p.

cup	hug	sun	jump
cut	rug	sunny	lump
but	bug	fun	hum
hut	dug	funny	son
huff	dust	run	done
puff	duck	rub	does

Read the following sentences aloud, slowly and carefully. Find the words containing the sound of u̲ as in u̲p.

1. It is fun to run and run.

2. The bug is on the rug.

3. Biddy Hen said, "Cluck! Cluck! Cluck!"

4. You must not touch the little duck.

5. The little bunny looks so funny.

6. The big bad wolf went huff, huff, huff.

7. The little engine went puff, puff, puff.

8. Rub, rub, rub, and scrub, scrub, scrub!

Write some additional sentences in your Work Book using the above word lists.

NOTE: The teacher should explain that various *other spellings* represent the sound of *u* as in *up*, for example: *son*, *does*, *blood*, *touch*.

DRILLS FOR VOWEL SOUNDS

8. Words Containing the Sound of <u>u</u> as in <u>burn</u>

Say these words slowly.   Listen for the sound of <u>u</u> as in <u>burn</u>.

turn	sir	dirt	word
turkey	fir	dirty	work
turtle	first	third	world
hurt	girl	thirty	worm
purr	bird	chirp	worth
fur	birdie	search	worse

Read the following sentences aloud, slowly and carefully.   Find the words containing the sound of <u>u</u> as in <u>burn</u>.

1. Jerry was playing with a girl near the church.

2. They heard some birds chirping.

3. At first they could not find the birds.

4. They searched and searched.

5. The birds chirped and chirped.

6. They turned around and saw four birds.

7. One bird was hurt.

8. Jerry picked him up and hurried home.

Write some additional sentences in your Work Book using the above word lists.

NOTE: The teacher should explain that various *other spellings* represent the sound of *u* as in *burn*, for example: her bird, word, learn, journal.

9. Words Containing the Sound of a as in about

Say these words slowly. Listen for the sound of <u>a</u> as in <u>about</u>.

ago	away	above	sofa
again	awake	asleep	banana
against	alike	across	collar
along	aloud	afraid	company
around	alone	agree	idea

Read the following sentences aloud, slowly and carefully. Find the words containing the sound of <u>a</u> as in <u>about</u>.

1. Ben found that little dog about a month ago.

2. The dog must have run away from home.

3. He was asleep in the park.

4. He was all alone.

5. When he awoke, he seemed to be afraid.

6. He ran around and around the park.

7. He jumped against the fence.

8. When we went home, he came along with us.

9. We tried again and again to find the owner.

Write some additional sentences in your Work Book using the above word lists.

10. Words Containing the Sound of e as in under

Say these words slowly. Listen for the sound of e as in under.

sister	supper	winter	butter
brother	dinner	summer	better
mother	faster	Easter	never
father	master	teacher	ever
farmer	rooster	after	feather

Read the following sentences aloud, slowly and carefully. Find the words containing the sound of e as in under.

1. My brother is going away this summer.

2. He is going away with my father's sister.

3. My father's sister is my aunt.

4. Last Easter, she came to visit my father.

5. We had a picnic supper in the woods.

6. My brother and I planned the supper.

7. Mother and father took us in the car.

8. After supper we walked to the farmer's house.

9. We bought a pound of butter from the farmer.

Write some additional sentences in your Work Book using the above word lists.

11. Words Containing the Sound of oo as in food

Say these words slowly.   Listen for the sound of oo as in food.

moon	do	too	blue
noon	who	two	true
soon	whom	goose	truth
spoon	whose	roof	drew
cool	soup	room	grew
school	shoe	broom	fruit

Read the following sentences aloud, slowly and carefully.   Find the words containing the sound of oo as in food.

1. Ruth goes to our school.

2. She has a blue dress, and a blue hat.

3. Ruth and I play in my playroom.

4. We play school every afternoon.

5. Ruth sits on a stool and is the teacher.

6. She says, "Add two and two."

7. "Two times two are four," Ruth says.

8. After school, we sweep the room.

Write some additional sentences in your Work Book using the above word lists.

NOTE: The teacher should explain that various *other spellings* represent the sound of *oo* as in *food*, for example: do, rude, group, blue, drew, fruit.

DRILLS FOR VOWEL SOUNDS **oo**

12. Words Containing the Sound of oo as in foot

Say these words slowly. Listen for the sound of oo as in foot.

book	good	could	put
cook	stood	should	push
cooky	wood	would	bush
took	hood	wool	bushel
look	brook	full	butcher
looked	shook	pull	sugar

Read the following sentences aloud, slowly and carefully. Find the words containing the sound of oo as in foot.

1. I have a book about Red Riding Hood.

2. Little Red Riding Hood lived near the woods.

3. The bushes in the woods were full of berries.

4. She picked a basket full for her grandmother.

5. There was a brook in the woods.

6. Near the brook stood a very large wolf.

7. Red Riding Hood took one look at the wolf.

8. Would you like to know more about the wolf?

Write some additional sentences in your Work Book using the above word lists.

NOTE: The teacher should explain that various *other spellings* represent the sound of oo as in *foot*, for example: wolf, full, would.

13. Words Containing the Sound of o̲ as in c̲o̲r̲n̲

Say these words slowly. Listen for the sound of o̲ as in c̲o̲r̲n̲.

born	all	saw	caught
horn	ball	paw	taught
horse	tall	raw	thought
or	fall	law	brought
nor	call	walk	ought
north	hall	talk	short

Read the following sentences aloud, slowly and carefully. Find the words containing the sound of o̲ as in c̲o̲r̲n̲.

1. All the boys in our room took a walk.

2. Shall we talk about the things the boys saw?

3. Ted saw some cows in the corn field.

4. Ben saw a horse with a very short tail.

5. Jack saw two small boys playing ball.

6. Dick saw a cat with a sore paw.

7. Ben may take the chalk and draw the horse.

8. Dick may draw the cat with the sore paw.

Write some additional sentences in your Work Book using the above word lists.

NOTE: The teacher should explain that various *other spellings* represent the sound of *o* as in *corn*, for example: *all, saw, caught, thought, broad.*

14. Words Containing the Sound of <u>o</u> as in <u>not</u>

Say these words slowly. Listen for the sound of <u>o</u> as in <u>not</u>.

got	rock	ox	bottle
pot	sock	box	cottage
hot	knock	boxes	collar
hop	lock	fox	dollar
top	block	foxes	follow
stop	clock	fond	hollow

Read the following sentences aloud, slowly and carefully. Find the words containing the sound of <u>o</u> as in <u>not</u>.

1. Hop! Hop! Hop! little froggie.

2. Stop! Stop! Stop! little bird.

3. Bob stood on the top of the rock.

4. He called, "Hop, hop, hop, little froggie."

5. He called, "Stop, stop, stop, little bird."

6. The little frog hopped and hopped.

7. The little bird would not stop.

8. The frog hopped away to the pond.

Write some additional sentences in your Work Book using the above word lists.

DRILLS FOR VOWEL SOUNDS

15. Words Containing the Sound of <u>a</u> as in <u>cart</u>

Say these words slowly. Listen for the sound of <u>a</u> as in <u>cart</u>.

car	are	tar	march
card	arm	star	market
far	part	start	marble
farm	park	smart	garden
farmer	bark	lark	yard
father	barn	large	heart

Read the following sentences aloud, slowly and carefully. Find the words containing the sound of <u>a</u> as in <u>cart</u>.

1. We will go to my father's farm in our car.

2. The car is in the yard.

3. Father says we will start at six o'clock.

4. We have a large barn on the farm.

5. A farmer takes care of the farm.

6. Father likes to work in the garden.

7. We take the flowers to the market in the car.

8. The farmer takes the vegetables in a large truck.

Write some additional sentences in your Work Book using the above word lists.

NOTE: The teacher should explain that various *other spellings* represent the sound of *a* as in *cart*, for example: h*ea*rt, c*a*lm.

16. Words Containing the Sound of <u>a</u> as in <u>make</u>

Say these words slowly. Listen for the sound of <u>a</u> as in <u>make</u>.

make	came	may	rain
bake	game	day	train
cake	same	say	sail
wake	name	stay	tail
take	age	lay	pail
lake	cage	play	paint

Read the following sentences aloud, slowly and carefully. Find the words containing the sound of <u>a</u> as in <u>make</u>.

1. James and Kate came on the train yesterday.

2. They came to stay ten days.

3. They have been painting almost all day today.

4. James painted the gate.

5. Kate painted the bird cage.

6. The bird cage is painted green, the gate blue.

7. James stopped painting to sail his boat on the lake.

8. Kate stayed at home and played with her dolls.

Write some additional sentences in your Work Book using the above word lists.

NOTE: The teacher should explain that various *other spellings* represent the sound of *a* as in *make*, for example: m*a*y, r*ai*n, br*ea*k, th*ey*.

17. Words Containing the Sound of i as in ice

Say these words slowly. Listen for the sound of <u>i</u> as in <u>ice</u>.

mice	ride	right	by
nice	hide	might	my
rice	side	light	why
kite	nine	night	cry
white	find	sight	pie
while	five	tight	tie

Read the following sentences aloud, slowly and carefully. Find the words containing the sound of <u>i</u> as in <u>ice</u>.

1. Billy has some white mice.

2. He had nine, but five got away.

3. It happened one night.

4. Billy and Bob were fighting.

5. While they were fighting, they upset the cage.

6. The mice ran outside.

7. They tried and tried to catch the mice.

8. They could not find five of the mice.

Write some additional sentences in your Work Book using the above word lists.

NOTE: The teacher should explain that various *other spellings* represent the sound of *i* as in *ice*, for example: b*y*, p*ie*, *eye*, h*eight*, *ai*sle.

18. Words Containing the Sound of <u>o</u> as in <u>old</u>

Say these words slowly. Listen for the sound of <u>o</u> as in <u>old</u>.

hold	nose	blow	boat
cold	rose	snow	coat
sold	road	know	goat
so	hope	row	soap
go	rope	grow	oak
goes	smoke	throw	throat

Read the following sentences aloud, slowly and carefully. Find the words containing the sound of <u>o</u> as in <u>old</u>.

1. "Oh! Oh! Oh!" said little Joe.

2. "May I roll in the snow?" said Joe.

3. "No! No! No!" said Joe's mother.

4. Your toes and nose will be cold.

5. Please hold my coat. I want to go.

6. You may go if you will not throw snowballs.

7. May we roll the snow for a snow man?

8. I will show you how to roll the snow.

Write some additional sentences in your Work Book using the above word lists.

NOTE: The teacher should explain that various *other spellings* represent the sound of *o* as in *old*, for example: *oh, blow, sew, boat.*

19. Words Containing the Sound of <u>ou</u> as in <u>round</u>

Say these words slowly.   Listen for the sound of <u>ou</u> as in <u>round</u>.

house	found	ow	down
mouse	sound	cow	town
mouth	ground	now	clown
south	loud	plow	brown
out	cloud	how	drown
shout	crowd	owl	crown

Read the following sentences aloud, slowly and carefully.   Find the words containing the sound of <u>ou</u> as in <u>round</u>.

1. Bob Brown saw a clown in town.

2. The crowd stood near the clown.

3. The brownie ran around the clown.

4. The crowd shouted and shouted.

5. "Bowwow! Bowwow!" said the dog.

6. The clown wore a funny crown.

7. He put the crown on the brownie.

8. The crown fell to the ground.

Write some additional sentences in your Work Book using the above word lists.

DRILLS FOR VOWEL SOUNDS

oi

20. Words Containing the Sound of <u>oi</u> as in <u>oil</u>

Say these words slowly. Listen for the sound of <u>oi</u> as in <u>oil</u>.

boy	boil	voice	noise
toy	boiled	choice	noisy
joy	soil	rejoice	poison
join	soiled	point	destroy
Joyce	spoil	pointed	employ
Roy	spoiled	appoint	annoy

Read the following sentences aloud, slowly and carefully. Find the words containing the sound of <u>oi</u> as in <u>oil</u>.

1. Roy is a boy in our school.

2. He was our choice for captain of our team.

3. The boys enjoy playing baseball.

4. Twelve boys joined the club.

5. Joyce is Roy's little sister.

6. Joyce has lots of toys.

7. She cries when Roy takes her toys.

8. Roy seems to enjoy teasing Joyce.

Write some additional sentences in your Work Book using the above word lists.

21. Words Containing the Sound of u as in use

Say these words slowly.   Listen for the sound of u as in use.

cute	new	beauty
cube	mew	future
tune	few	value
tulip	knew	huge
pupil	dew	human
music	duty	Hugh

Read the following sentences aloud, slowly and carefully.   Find the words containing the sound of u as in use.

1. The new pupil in our room is named Hugh.

2. Hugh came to school a few days ago.

3. He was wearing a beautiful new suit.

4. Hugh is taking music lessons.

5. The music teacher comes during school.

6. Hugh brought some beautiful tulips to school.

7. Hugh has a little kitten at home.

8. The kitten says, "Mew, Mew, Mew."

Write some additional sentences in your Work Book using the above word lists.

NOTE: The teacher should explain that various *other spellings* represent the sound of *u* as in *use*, for example: *new, view, beautiful.*

DRILLS FOR VOWELS

22. Vowel Sounds for Use in Vocal Exercises

1. ah
   ay
   ee
   aw
   oh
   oo

2. ah ay
      ay ee
         ee aw
            aw oh
               oh oo

3. ah ay ee
      ay ee aw
         ee aw oh
            aw oh oo

4. ah ay ee aw
      ay ee aw oh
         ee aw oh oo

5. ah ay ee aw oh
      ay ee aw oh oo

6. ah ay ee aw oh oo

NOTE: The above vowel sounds, *ah* as in *arm*, *a* as in *may*, *ee* as in *see*, *aw* as in *saw*, *oh* as in *old*, *oo* as in *moon*, may be used in various types of vocal exercises. They may be combined with any consonant as: *pah, pay, pee;* or *sah say, say see* etc.; or any consonant blend, as: *blah, blay, blee*, etc. These exercises should preferably be used under the guidance of teacher familiar with speech correction practice.

KEY TO VOWELS

To the teacher: Vowels are classified according to *A Guide to Pronunciation, Merriam-Webster New International Dictionary-1935*. The page numbers refer to practice exercises for the designated vowel sounds. The exercises include the vowel sounds which are used most frequently in the elementary grades.

		Page
a	as in make, same, day, rain	127
a	as in care, share, air, chair, bear	115
a	as in at, add, hat, happy	116
a	as in cart, far, star, father	126
a	as in ask,[1] dance, past, last	117
a	as in about, around, company, collar, sofa	120
a	as in all, saw, talk; (see o)	124
a	as in any, said, says; (see e)	114
au	as in caught, taught; (see o)	124
e	as in he, sheep, eat, key	112
e	as in egg, end, red, head	114
e	as in under, dinner, farmer, ever	121
e	as in her, heard, earth; (see u)	119
i	as in ice, night, time, five	128
i	as in it, ill, pig, city (citi)	113
i	as in girl, bird, first, third (see u)	119
o	as in old, boat, grow, oh	129
o	as in corn, horse, north, thought	124
o	as in not, hot, block, porridge	125
oi	as in oil, boil, boy (boi), joy (joi)	131
oo	as in food, moon, school, room	122

[1] "The symbol å is used to represent an a sound somewhat variable in quality, intermediate between ă in man and ä in art, and medium or long in duration." .... In standard speech three different pronunciations are current in the "a as in ask" group of words: ă as in măn, ä as in art, or å as in ask, as above. A separate grouping of these words is offered for use, but "the problem of the correct use of the sounds ă, å, and ä for this group is chiefly one of consistency."—*A Guide to Pronunciation, Merriam-Webster.*

KEY TO VOWELS—continued

ARTICULATION TEST MATERIAL

Directions for Giving Test
Speech Diagnostic Chart
Key to Diagnostic Sentences

DIRECTIONS FOR GIVING ARTICULATION TEST

For the Identification of Consonant and Vowel Errors in Speech

The examiner should keep in mind that the child who is to be tested may have a serious speech defect, toward which he may have emotional reactions which increase his difficulty in speaking, especially under unusual circumstances. Since the test is to determine the articulatory defects which appear in the pupil's speech when he is speaking in his accustomed manner, the examiner should make every effort to give the pupil a feeling of confidence. During the test no comment should be made on any word incorrectly pronounced but if the pupil is unable to recognize a word the examiner should supply it and ask the pupil to repeat the sentence again.

1. Material for Testing

Two copies of *Better Speech and Better Reading* should be provided. The pupil should read aloud the *Diagnostic Sentences* on page 2, while the examiner uses the *Key to the Diagnostic Sentences* on page 141 as a guide. Opposite the *Key* appears the *Diagnostic Chart-Articulation Test* which is used for recording the errors appearing in the pupil's speech.

2. Explanation of Key to the Diagnostic Sentences

Numbers on the *Key to the Diagnostic Sentences* correspond to the numbers on the *Diagnostic Sentences*, and to the numbers on the *Diagnostic Chart-Articulation Test*. Each sentence tests a particular sound. The sound to be tested appears at the left of the sentence, and in the sentence in bold face type. Consonants are tested in their initial, medial, and final positions, and in the most frequently used blends, as:

Sentence 15.   l   A **l**ady gave us the tu**l**ips in that bow**l**.
      44. st   I **st**ay up**st**airs in the be**st** room in our house.

Vowels to be tested appear at least three times in a sentence, as :

Sentence 76.   e   H**e** saw a sh**ee**p asl**ee**p in the field.

3. Use of Speech Diagnostic Chart.

The small index numbers on the *Diagnostic Chart-Articulation Test* (p. 140) correspond to the numbers on the *Diagnostic Sentences, Key to the Diagnostic Sentences*, and *Diagnostic Test Words*. The pupil should be asked to read aloud the sentences on page 2. Using the "Key" as guide, the examiner should listen carefully to the pronunciation of each designated sound. For example, a pupil may read sentence 15, "A lady gave us the tulips in that bowl," as "A **w**ady gave us the tu**w**ips in that bow." In this instance it should be noted that the sound of l is incorrectly pronounced in its initial and medial positions, and omitted in its final position. The error should therefore be indicated on the *Diagnostic Chart* by an x, as

	Initial	Medial	Final
15l	×	×	×

Caution: If a pupil has very defective speech more than one defective sound may appear in a given sentence. This sometimes causes confusion to the inexperienced examiner. If it is borne in mind that only one sound is being *tested* in each sentence, and all other defects in the sentence disregarded, the examiner should have no difficulty in marking the chart. The reverse side of the chart may be used for a brief case history.

4. Use of Diagnostic Test Words

Numbers on the *Diagnostic Test Words* (page 6) correspond to those on the *Diagnostic Chart*. It should be noted that this test is less complete than that given by the *Diagnostic Sentences*, since it tests only the initial and final sounds. The pupil should be asked to read, or repeat, either one or more of the Test Words in a group. The examiner should record any error on the *Diagnostic Chart* as noted in paragraph 3 above.

5. Use of Phonovisual Diagnostic Consonant and Vowel Chart

These charts (pages 11a and 11b) may be used to test the child who has not yet learned to read. Only the initial sound is tested, except in final ng and x. Index numbers on the chart correspond to the numbers on the Articulation Test of the Speech Diagnostic Chart.

Speech Diagnostic Chart*

School_____ Grade_____

Name_____ Date of Birth_____

Address_____

Date of Test_____ Corrected_____

Remarks:

_____
_____
_____
_____
_____
_____
_____
_____
_____
_____
_____
_____
_____
_____
_____
_____
_____
_____
_____
_____
_____
_____
_____
_____

Examined by_____

Teacher.

*For the identification of consonant and vowel errors in speech. (See reverse side.)

Diagnostic Chart*—Articulation Test

Initial	Medial	Final	Initial	Medial	Final	Initial	Medial	Final	Initial	Medial	Final	Initial	Medial	Final	Initial	Medial	Final	Vowels	Vowels
1 p			15 l			26 r			39 s			53 z			67 k			76 ē	89 ā
2 b			16 bl		—	27 br		—	40 sk		—	54		bz	68	lk		77 Ĭ	90 Ĭ
3 m			17 cl			28 cr		—	41 sm		—	55		dz	69 qu			78 ŏ	91 ð
4 wh		—	18 fl		—	29 dr		—	42 sn			56		lz	70 squ			79 å	92 ou
5 w		—	19 gl		—	30 fr		—	43 sp		—	57		mz	71	x (ks)		80 ă	93 oi
6 f			20 pl		—	31 gr		—	44 st		—	58		nz	72 g			81 ŭ	94 ū
7 v			21 sl		—	32 pr		—	45 sw			59		ngz	73	x (gz)		82 û	
8 th			22 spl	—	—	33 scr		—	46		fs	60		thz	74	ng		83 à	
9 th			23		dl	34 shr	—	—	47		ls	61		vz	75 h			84 ōō	
10 t			24		tl	35 spr		—	48		ns	62 sh						85 ŏŏ	
11 tw	—	—	25		zl	36 str		—	49		ps	63	zh					86 ô	
12 d						37 tr		—	50		ts	64 ch						87 ǒ	
13 dw	—	—				38 thr	—	—	51		sts	65 j						88 ä	
14 n									52		ths	66 y	—						

* Note: Numbers on the chart correspond to numbers of the Diagnostic Sentences, Diagnostic Test Words, and Phonovisual Vowel and Consonant Charts. For directions for giving Articulation Test, see page 138 and page 12.

For the convenience of the teacher reprints of this chart, designed to fit a standard loose-leaf notebook are obtainable from the publisher in packages of 50.

ARTICULATION TEST

Key to Diagnostic Sentences*

(Do not let the pupil see this page)

Test for Consonants

1.	**p**	The girl *p*ut the pa*p*er on to*p* of the table.
2.	**b**	The *b*oy put the ba*b*y in the tu*b*.
3.	**m**	The *m*an saw the far*m*er at the far*m*.
4.	**wh**	Please put the *wh*eel some*wh*ere else.
5.	**w**	*W*e are going a*w*ay on Monday.
6.	**f**	The *f*armer has a beautiful cal*f*.
7.	**v**	The *v*illage by the ri*v*er is fi*v*e miles away.
8.	**th**	I *th*ink his bir*th*day is next mon*th*.
9.	**th**	*Th*at mo*th*er will go wi*th* her son.
10.	**t**	I *t*old her your le*tt*er had no*t* come.
11.	**tw**	*Tw*enty boys stood be*tw*een the houses.
12.	**d**	*D*id Da*dd*y ri*d*e the horse?
13.	**dw**	The *dw*arf lives in the wood.
14.	**n**	Do *n*ot give mo*n*ey to that ma*n*.

---

* For use of key, see page 138.

15.	l	A *l*ady gave us the tu*l*ips in that bow*l*.
16.	bl	The *bl*ack bunny is nib*bl*ing a carrot.
17.	cl	The *cl*own de*cl*ared he was sick.
18.	fl	The *fl*ying snow*fl*akes are beautiful.
19.	gl	I am *gl*ad my looking-*gl*ass wasn't broken.
20.	pl	*Pl*ease look at the air*pl*ane I made.
21.	sl	The *sl*y boy seemed to be a*sl*eep.
22.	spl	The baby *spl*ashed in her tub.
23.	-dl	The baby is in the cra*dl*e.
24.	-tl	The boy caught a tur*tl*e.
25.	-zl	He has a new puz*zl*e.
26.	r	The *r*abbit ate a ca*r*rot.
27.	br	*Br*ing your um*br*ella with you.
28.	cr	She heard the baby *cr*ying a*cr*oss the road.
29.	dr	Please *dr*aw a picture for the chil*dr*en.
30.	fr	My *fr*iend is not a*fr*aid.
31.	gr	*Gr*andma gives me cake when I am hun*gr*y.
32.	pr	The *pr*ince sur*pr*ised the king.
33.	scr	She *scr*eamed when he de*scr*ibed the fight.
34.	shr	We have some *shr*ubs in our yard.
35.	spr	I like the *spr*ing of the year.
36.	str	The *str*eet car de*str*oyed the bicycle.
37.	tr	I shall *tr*y to go to the coun*tr*y on Monday.
38.	thr	He has *thr*ee books for you.

39.	s	I *s*aw the poli*c*eman near our hou*s*e.
40.	**sk**	The *sch*ool ba*sk*et is by my de*sk*.
41.	**sm**	I saw the *sm*oke.
42.	**sn**	I like to play in the *sn*ow.
43.	**sp**	Although I *sp*oke in a whi*sp*er it made her ga*sp*.
44.	**st**	He *st*ayed up*st*airs in the gue*st* room.
45.	**sw**	*Sw*ing high, swing low, and over you'll go.
46.	**-fs**	When she reads that story, she lau*ghs*.
47.	**-ls**	No one e*ls*e will be here.
48.	**-ns**	She saw him only o*nc*e.
49.	**-ps**	Where are the blue cu*ps*?
50.	**-ts**	Mary has two new ha*ts*.
51.	**-sts**	Daddy has two white ve*sts*.
52.	**-ths**	Were you away the last two mon*ths*?
53.	**z**	*Z*ell came Thur*s*day with the boy*s*.
54.	**-bz**	Look at the spider we*bs*.
55.	**-dz**	He has many frien*ds*.
56.	**-lz**	Where are the other gir*ls*?
57.	**-mz**	Did you bring both dru*ms*?
58.	**-nz**	I play in the house when it rai*ns*.
59.	**-ngz**	We learned two new so*ngs*.
60.	**-thz**	He tore his clo*thes*.
61.	**-vz**	I will show you where Bob li*ves*.

62.	**sh**	I *sh*all sit in the sun*sh*ine near the bu*sh*.
63.	**-zh**	Father put his car as u*s*ual in our gara*g*e.
64.	**ch**	The *ch*ild saw his tea*ch*er in chur*ch*.
65.	**j**	*J*ack has a pi*g*eon in a ca*g*e.
66.	**y**	Do *y*ou like on*i*ons?
67.	**k**	*C*ome and see the mon*k*ey in my boo*k*.
68.	**-lk**	After mi*lk*ing the cow, put the mi*lk* in the can.
69.	**qu**	The *qu*een re*qu*ested the king to see the man.
70.	**squ**	The *squ*irrel is in the cage.
71.	**-x(-ks)**	All the boys are here e*x*cept Ma*x*.
72.	**g**	We shall *g*o in the wa*g*on to get the do*g*.
73.	**-x(-gz)**	Those are e*x*actly the right fla*g*s.
74.	**-ng**	She was swi*ng*ing in our swi*ng*.
75.	**h**	*H*e hid be*h*ind the house.

Test for Vowels

76.   ē   H*e* saw a sh*ee*p asl*ee*p in the f*ie*ld.

77.   ĭ   D*i*d you buy the r*i*ng *i*n our c*i*ty?

78.   ĕ   The little r*e*d h*e*n laid an *e*gg in the n*e*st.

79.   â   Th*e*re is the best ch*air* for Baby B*ear*.

80.   ă   Th*a*t f*a*t m*a*n looks very h*a*ppy.

81.   ŭ   She c*u*t the bread and b*u*ttered it for l*u*nch.

82.   û   Her b*ir*d was h*ur*t when the cage t*ur*ned over.

83.   *a*̇   He paid *a*bout a doll*a*r for his dog's coll*a*r.

84.   ōo   He dr*ew* a picture of the st*oo*l in our r*oo*m.

85.   ŏŏ   She p*u*t the b*oo*k where he c*ou*ld see it.

86.   ô   Dan c*au*ght *a*ll the h*o*rses in the c*o*rnfield.

87.   ŏ   Do n*o*t dr*o*p the h*o*t p*o*rridge.

88.   ä   How f*ar* is your g*a*rden from our b*ar*n?

89.   ā   Th*ey* c*a*me on the tr*ai*n the other d*ay*.

90.   ī   My ch*i*ld will be f*i*ve by the t*i*me school opens.

91.   ō   It is s*o* c*o*ld I h*o*pe you will wear your c*o*at.

92.   ou   H*ow* did you get the cat *ou*t of the h*ou*se?

93.   oi   The b*oy* s*oi*led his hands with *oi*l.

94.   ū   H*u*gh has a b*eau*tiful t*u*lip.

NOTE: The diacritical marks are from the New Merriam-Webster International Dictionary—Second Edition.

POEMS

Peter, Peter

Peter, Peter, pumpkin eater,
Had a wife and couldn't keep her,
He put her in a pumpkin shell,
And there he kept her very well.

—Mother Goose

The Lollypops

There was a great commotion
  On the counter in the shop;
The lollypops got angry
  And they all began to pop.

They popped upon the counter,
  And they popped upon the floor;
They popped right out the window
  And they popped right out the door.

And everybody ran away,
  As fast as he could go.
For who would want a lollypop
  To chase one, don't you know?

—Cordia Thomas

Company

We hid up on the landing
near the top of the stairs,
and peeped through the railing
at people in their chairs.

We saw the tops of noses,
the tops of lips and cheeks,
and how a chin goes choppy
when anybody speaks.

We saw the tops of eyebrows,
and heads without a hat . . .
it's funny to see people
from the top-of-them, like that.

—Aileen Fisher

Little Raindrops

Oh, where do you come from,
  You little drops of rain,
Pitter patter, pitter patter,
  Down the window pane?

Tell me, little raindrops,
  Is that the way you play,
Pitter patter, pitter patter,
  All the rainy day?

The little raindrops cannot speak,
  But "pitter, patter pat"
Means, "We can play on this side,
  Why can't you play on that?"

—Ann Hawkshaw

If I Had a Pony

If I had a pony, a little yellow pony,
  With a green and golden saddle, and a silver bell to ring,
I'd mount him, and ride him along the merry highway
  Until I found the palace of his Majesty, the King.

And I'd say to the king, "I've a pretty, yellow pony
  With a tinkling silver bell, and a saddle, gold and green,
And I'd like to show my pony, and his bell, and his saddle
  To the prettiest little princess the world has ever seen."

And the king would answer kindly, "I'm sure she'd be delighted."
  And he'd send for the princess to come outside and see,
And I'd show her my pony, and I'd gallop him, and trot him,
  And I'm sure that she'd be eager to take a ride with me.

So I'd lift her up before me, and we'd gallop off together
  And never a man could catch us, so swiftly would we ride,
And we'd leave the town behind us, and along the merry highway
  I'd bring the pretty princess home to be my little bride.

—Gorton Veeder Carruth

* NOTE: For additional poems for "p," see page 205.

The Bug and the Beetle

Little Black Beetle said one day,
"Little bug, you're in my way!
Little bug, don't bother me,
I'm a big bug, don't you see?"
Little bug said, "I can do
Quite as many things as you."
—Unknown

Budding Trees

The budding trees are bending down,
   And bowing very low,
The wind is making them say good-bye
   As they watch the winter go.

The trees are waving their branches now,
   And robins fly in and sing.
The trees in the wind all wave their hands
   And throw a kiss to spring.
—Mildred Evans

Group 2. b—continued*

The Sky Is a Blue, Blue Sea

The sky is a blue, blue sea,
　The moon is a silver boat,
The stars are water-lilies
　On the blue, blue sea afloat.

Let's off on the silver boat,
　And away to dreamland go,
And gather happy dreams
　In the garden where they grow.

—Mrs. Isla Paschal Richardson

A Hint to the Wise

I know a little garden path
　That leads you through the trees,
Past flower-beds and hollyhocks
　And by the homes of bees.
Until at last it brings you to
　A little fountain bath
Where tiny birds may wash themselves.
　If you go down that path,
Remember to be careful what
　You say. A little bird
May cause a deal of trouble by
　Repeating what he's heard.

—Pringle Barret

---

* NOTE: For additional poems for "b," see page 205.

Group 3. m*

A Humming Bee

One morning in the garden
  I heard a humming bee;
I sat awhile and listened
  While he hummed songs to me.
He hummed about the blue sky
  That stretches overhead,
He hummed about the fountains
  And what the fishes said.
He hummed about the nectar
  That makes the honey sweet,
And of the flowers nodding—
  Then hummed off down the street!
          —Wilhemina Seegmiller

The Birches

The little birches, white and slim,
Gleaming in the forest dim,
Must think the day is almost gone,
For each one has her nightie on.
          —Walter Prichard Eaton

* NOTE: For additional poems for "m," see page 205.

The Clouds

White sheep, white sheep,
  On a blue hill,
When the wind stops,
  You all stand still.

You walk far away,
  When the winds blow;
White sheep, white sheep,
  Where do you go?

      —Christina G. Rossetti

Whistles

I want to learn to whistle.
  I've always wanted to.
I fix my mouth to do it but
  The whistle won't come through.

I think perhaps it's stuck, and so
  I try it once again.
Can people swallow whistles?
  Where is my whistle then?

      —Dorothy Aldis

The Wonderful World

Great, wide, beautiful, wonderful world,
With the wonderful water round you curled,
And the wonderful grass upon your breast—
World! You are beautifully dressed!

The wonderful air is over me
And the wonderful wind is shaking the tree,
It walks on the water, and whirls the mills,
And talks to itself on the tops of the hills.

—William Brightly Rands

Which?

Whenever I'm walking in a wood
I'm never certain whether I should
Shuffle along where the dead leaves fall
Or walk as if I'm not there at all.

It's nice to rustle as hard as you can,
But I can't decide if it's nicer than
Creeping along, while the woodbirds call,
Pretending you are not there at all!

—Joyce L. Brisley

Under the Window

Under the window is my garden,
    Where sweet, sweet flowers grow;
And in the pear-tree dwells a robin,
    The sweetest bird I know.

—Kate Greenaway

Whistle

Can you whittle a whistle out of wood?
I wish you could,
I wish you would,
For a whistle whittled out of wood
Will do you worlds and worlds of good
If you blow with a will on your sunny way
Through the glow of dawn and the glare of day.

O whittle a whistle of willow wood!
I think you could,
I know you should.
Then play a tune in a merry mood,
A lilting tune through the drooping wood,
With notes as clear as the call of the lark
Through shadows of twilight and the dark.

—Leonard Twynham

---

* Note: For additional poems for "wh" and "w," see page 205.

Goldfish

I have four fish with poppy eyes,
Awfully poppy for their size,—
Perhaps they're poppy from surprise:

For after frisking in a sea,
Fish must find it queer to be
Looking through a glass at ME.

     —Aileen Fisher

Fireflies

I wonder if the fireflies
 Are baby stars that fall,
And come to make the lonely earth
 A friendly little call.

     —Helen Virginia Frey

Fire in the Window

Fire in the window! Flashes in the
   pane!
Fire on the roof-top! blazing
   weather vane!
Turn about, weather vane! put the
   fire out!
The sun's going down, sir, I haven't
   a doubt.

     —Mary Mapes Dodge

---

* NOTE: For additional poems for "f," see page 205.

Group 6. v

I Have a Doll

I have a doll, I have a book,
  I have a big white ball;
I have a ring, I have a toy,
  I have a place for all.

I have a gun, I have a dog,
  I have a rubber ball,
I have a train, I have a wheel.
  I'm glad I have them all.
            —Unknown

As I Was Going to St. Ives

As I was going to St. Ives,
I met a man with seven wives,
Each wife had seven sacks,
Each sack had seven cats,
Each cat had seven kits,
Kits, cats, sacks, and wives,
How many were going to St. Ives?
            —Old Rime

Hiding

I have a cave of grapevines
   With walls of rustling leaves,
With willow branches for a roof
   And ivy vines for eaves.

I have a private place there
   Behind a leafy screen
Where I can watch the people pass
   And never once be seen.
               —Aileen Fisher

Keeping Store

We have bags and bags of whitest down
   Out of the milk-weed pods;
We have purple asters in lovely heaps,
   And stacks of golden-rods.

We have needles out of the sweet pine woods,
   And spools of cobweb thread,
We have bachelor's buttons for dolly's dress
   And hollyhock caps for her head.
              —Mary F. Butts

* NOTE: For additional poems for "v," see page 205.

Thirty Thousand Thoughtless Boys

Thirty thousand thoughtless boys
Thought they'd make a thundering noise;
So with thirty thousand thumbs,
They thumped on thirty thousand drums.

—Unknown

The Package

There's a package,
There's a package,
There's a package in the mail.
It's wrapped in yellow paper
And the twine is like a tail.
Three stamps are in the corner—
One red, the others pale.
There's a package,
There's a package,
There's a package in the mail.

It's for mother,
It's for mother,
It's for mother, I can see.
But that is just about as good
As knowing it's for me,
For mother'll say, "Come, open it,
Untie the string and see!"
There's a package,
There's a package . . .
Oh, what CAN the package be?

—Aileen Fisher

The Old Woman

There was an old woman
   And nothing she had;
And so this old woman
   Was said to be mad.
She'd nothing to eat,
   She'd nothing to wear,
She'd nothing to lose,
   She'd nothing to fear,
She'd nothing to ask,
   And nothing to give,
And when she did die,
   She'd nothing to leave.

           —Unknown

A Bunch of Roses

The rosy mouth and rosy toe
   Of little baby brother
Until about a month ago
   Had never met each other;
But nowadays the neighbors sweet,
   In every sort of weather,
Half way with rosy fingers meet,
   To kiss and play together.

          —John Bannister Tabb

A Game of Tag

A grasshopper once had a game of tag
  With some crickets that lived near by,
When he stubbed his toe, and over he went
  Too quick to see with your eye.

Then the crickets leaned up against a fence,
  And chirped till their sides were sore,
But the grasshopper said, "You are laughing at me,
  And I won't play any more."

So off he went though he wanted to stay,
  For he was not hurt by the fall,
And the gay little crickets went on with the game,
  And never missed him at all.

                —Unknown

Our Two Gardens

We have two gardens. One is sweet
With flowers, and one grows things to eat.
My father calls them, just for fun,
The Mary and the Martha one.

                —Richard Kirk

Group 7. th—continued*

The Dearest Land

What country is most dear of all
    Beneath the heaven's blue?
The dearest land is one's own land,
    Go search the wide world through.
                  —Edmund Clarence Stedman

Yours and Mine

The sun, the trees, the grass, the sky,
The silver moon that's sailing by,
The rain and dew and snowflakes white,
The flowers sweet and stars of night!

The songs of birds, wind whispering,
The autumn leaves, the buds of spring—
Such lovely things to hear and see
Belong to you, belong to me!
                  —Frances Gorman Risser

New Year Prayer

Dear God, this New Year I will give thanks to Thee
For beautiful everyday things I can see:
The sky, a red sunset, pale clouds floating by,
Gold leaves of the fall, winter snow piling high,
Spring flowers, brown wood paths, and evergreen trees,
The new moon, and twilight, tall grass in a breeze.
In each day before me some new beauty lies.
To see Thee, I need only open my eyes!
                  —Mildred Evans

---

* Note: For additional poems for "th," see page 205.

The Clock

Tick, tock, tick, tock,
Merrily sings the clock;
It's time for work,
It's time for play,
So it sings throughout the day.
Tick, tock, tick, tock,
Merrily sings the clock.

—Unknown

Night Blessing

Good night,
Sleep tight,
Wake up bright
In the morning light
To do what's right
With all your might.

—Old Saying

Twink! Twink!

Twink, twink, twink, twink,
    Twinkety, twinkety, twink!
The fireflies light their lanterns,
    Then put them out in a wink,

Twink, twink, twink, twink!
    They light their lights once more
Then twinkety, twinkety, twink, twink!
    They put them out as before.

—Wilhemina Seegmiller

* NOTE: For additional poems for "t," see page 205.

The Two Dogs

Two little dogs
Sat by the fire,
Beside a scuttle of coal-dust;
Said one little dog
To the other little dog,
"If you don't talk, why I must."
—Old Rime

Fairy Umbrellas

Out in the waving meadow grass
  The pretty daisies grow,
I love to see their golden eyes,
  Their petals white as snow.
I wonder if the fairies use
  The dainty little flowers,
To keep their frocks from getting wet
  In sudden April showers.
—Lucy Diamond

---

* NOTE: For additional poems for "d," see page 206.

Group 10. n*

November

No shade, no shine,
No butterflies, no bees,
No fruits, no flowers,
No leaves, no birds,
November!

—Unknown

Jack O'Lantern

The Man in the Moon looked down on the field,
    Where the golden pumpkin lay;
He winked at him, and he blinked at him,
    In the funniest kind of way.

But on Hallowe'en, when the moon looked down
    From the sky, through the shadows dim,
The pumpkin fat on a gatepost sat,
    And saucily laughed at him.

—Anna Chandler Ayer

Logic

I have a copper penny and another copper penny,
    Well, then, of course, I have two copper pence;
I have a cousin Jenny and another cousin Jenny,
    Well, pray, then, do I have two cousin Jence?

—Unknown

---

* NOTE: For additional poems for "n," see page 206.

The Lamplighter

My tea is nearly ready and the sun
  has left the sky;
It's time to take the window to see
  Leerie going by:
For every night at tea-time and before
  you take your seat,
With lantern and with ladder he comes
  posting up the street.

For we are very lucky, with a lamp
  before the door,
And Leerie stops to light it as he
  lights so many more;
And O! before you hurry by with
  ladder and with light
O Leerie, see a little child and
  nod to him tonight!

             —Robert Louis Stevenson

Little Wind

Little wind, blow on the hilltop;
  Little wind, blow down the plain;
Little wind, blow up the sunshine;
  Little wind, blow off the rain.
          —Kate Greenaway

Group 11. 1—continued

The Lonely Goldfish

I have a goldfish in a bowl
  A lonely little fellow,
With nothing in the world to do
  But stay there, and be yellow.

—Alicia Aspinwall

Bird Language

The little birdie on this tree
Is singing sweetly now for me.
I'm sure he's glad the livelong day,
His songs are all so bright and gay.

Once when a bird was singing loud,
I told him I would be so proud
If only I his language knew—
But off the little birdie flew.

—Florence B. Steiner

Easter

The air is like a butterfly
  With frail blue wings.
The happy earth looks at the sky
  And sings.

—Joyce Kilmer

April Music

I'd like to spend April
Sitting on a hill,
With a mushroom for a parasol
And violets for a frill.

And the wind for a violin
To play spring tunes,
And the blossoms in the treetops
For gay balloons.

I'd like to spend April
Sitting on a mound
Watching for the flowers to pop
Out of the ground.

With their green silk stockings
And their new spring clothes,
Trying to look taller
By dancing on their toes!

—Aileen Fisher

Our Flag

Red as a rose,
  Blue as the sky,
White as the clouds
  Floating on high.

—Unknown

Fall

I like fall:
it always smells smoky,
the chimneys wake early,
the sun is poky;

Folks go past
in a hustle and bustle,
and when I walk
in the leaves, they rustle.

I like fall:
all the hills are hazy,
and after a frost
the puddles look glazy;

And nuts rattle down
where nobody's living,
and pretty soon . . .
it will be Thanksgiving!

—Aileen Fisher

October

October! O, October!
  I love your sparkling days,
Your gift of brilliant color,
  Your soft gray haze.

I love your fiery maples,
  I love your chestnut browns,
And all the sumac ladies
  In their gay red gowns.

I love the ripe corn standing
  In shocks so straight and bold,
I love the brown fields, resting,
  And the pumpkins clad in gold.

The orange of the bittersweet,
  The lovely gentian's blue,
The russet robes of sleepy ferns,
  I love your every hue.

October! O, October!
  I love your sparkling days.
Where do you find these wondrous tints
  That set the world ablaze?

—J. Evelyn Willoughby

Group 11. 1—continued

The Best Tree

Last summer I liked to stand under the trees.
The leaves blew about in the breezes like lace.
The trees in the autumn were lovelier still;
Red and gold leaves flying down in my face!
Now the evergreen tree that grows just by the gate
Is shining and twinkling and dazzling with light.
It's prettier far than all other trees are.
It's lighted to say "Merry Christmas" tonight.

—Mildred Evans

Christmas Bells

I heard a bell ring far away,
The happy bell of Christmas day:
Soon other bells took up the chime
To tell the world of Christmas time.
From belfries high and towers tall
The silver notes began to fall,
Till all the world rose glad and gay
To greet another Christmas day.

—Frances Kirkland

Song for Twelfth Night

Lavender's blue, dilly, dilly, lavender's green
When I am King, dilly, dilly, you shall be Queen;
Call up your men, dilly, dilly, set them to work:
Some to the plow, dilly, dilly, some to the cart,
Some to make hay, dilly, dilly, some to thresh corn:
Whilst you and I, dilly, dilly, keep ourselves warm.

—Unknown

Where the Fairies Dwell

Where, oh where, do the fairies dwell?
Under the ferns in the dingle dell,
In the violet blue 'neath the fairy fall,
On the sweet pea vine by the wobbly wall,
In the blue bell's cup by the rollicking rill,
In the daisy's crown on the heathery hill,
Deep in the wood where Sweet William springs,
Under the tips of the windflower's wings,
Where, oh where, do the fairies dwell?
Go to the flowers, for they know well.

—Nina Willis Walter

* NOTE: For additional poems for "l," see page 206.

Group 12. r

Rain

The rain is raining all around,
It falls on field and tree,
It rains on the umbrellas here,
And on the ships at sea.
—Robert Louis Stevenson

Little Robin Redbreast

Little Robin Redbreast sat upon a tree.
Up went pussy cat, down flew he.
Down came pussy cat,
Away Robin ran
Says little Robin Redbreast,
"Catch me if you can."
—Unknown

There Was a Crooked Man

There was a crooked man, and he went a crooked mile;
He found a crooked sixpence against a crooked stile;
He bought a crooked cat, which caught a crooked mouse,
And they all lived together in a little crooked house.
—Mother Goose

The Robin's Song

Robin is singing, a song of cheer,
Telling us that the spring is here,
High in the top of an old oak tree,
His tiny throat is bursting with glee.
Hark! he is singing, cheerie, cheerie.
Happy springtime is here, cheerie!

—Unknown

A Riddle

I creep on the ground and the children say:
"You ugly old thing," and push me away.
I lie in my bed and the children say:
"The fellow is dead; we'll throw him away."
At last I awake, and the children try
To make me stay as I rise and fly.

—Unknown

Group 12. r—continued*

Winter

Bread and milk for breakfast,
And woolen frocks to wear,
And a crumb for robin redbreast
On the cold days of the year.

—Christina G. Rossetti

About a Lion Named John

He's a black-maned lion,
Cross as sticks.
He eats a horse
Right while he kicks.
He eats a rhinoceros
(All but the horn),
And he gobbles zebras
As sure as you're born.
He eats a great
Long-necked giraffe,
And looks around for the other half.
Maybe you think
He's only John;
But you'd better keep
Your running shoes on!

—Gertrude duBois

---

* NOTE: For additional poems for "r," see page 206.

A Chinese Nursery Rhyme

He ran up the candlestick,
  The little mousey brown,
To steal and eat tallow,
  And he couldn't get down.
He called for his grandma
  But his grandma was in town;
So he doubled up into a wheel
  And rolled himself down.

—Translated by I. T. Headland

The Goldfish

My darling little goldfish
  Hasn't any toes;
He swims around without a sound
  And bumps his hungry nose.

He can't get out to play with me,
  Nor I get in to him,
Although I say: "Come out and play."
  And he—"Come in and swim."

—Dorothy Aldis

Group 13. s̲ and z̲—continued

If I Were an Elephant

If I had an elephant's floppy ears;
I'd wash them once in seven years;
I'd use my trunk for a garden hose
And make a nozzle out of my nose.

—Merle Crowell

"Lost"*

Have you seen a little dog
With a big brass collar?
He's mine!
He's lost!
The reward's one dollar!

If you happen to see him
Or hear him around
Telephone!
Quickly!
And tell me he's found.

He's a nice little dog
With a big brass collar.
He's mine!
He's lost!
The reward's one dollar!

—Alfred I. Tooke

---

* Taken by permission from *Recitation Stunts for Little Folks*,
published by Eldridge Entertainment House, Franklin, Ohio, price 50¢.

The Zebra at the Zoo

I saw a zebra
At the Zoo;
He couldn't say Z,
And he didn't bray,
And there wasn't much sense
To him any way.
His stripes just kept
On going 'round—
Yards and yards,
If he'd unwound.
But he couldn't say Z,
And he didn't bray;
And there wasn't much sense
To him any way.

—Gertrude duBois

A Swarm of Bees

A swarm of bees in May
Is worth a load of hay;
A swarm of bees in June
Is worth a silver spoon;
A swarm of bees in July
Is not worth a fly.

—Old Rime

The Man in the Moon

The Man in the Moon, as he sails the sky,
  Is a very remarkable skipper;
But he made a mistake when he tried to take
  A drink of milk from the Dipper.
He dipped it into the Milky Way,
  And slowly and carefully filled it;
The Big Bear growled, and the Little Bear howled,
  And scared him so that he spilled it.

—Old Rime

Unnatural History

The cuckoo in his little house
Keeps just as quiet as a mouse,
Excepting every hour, when he
Peeps out to see what he can see.
Our cat has tried for days and days
To catch him in all sorts of ways,
But always just a jiff before,
Old Tommy springs, he slams the door.
And that, as anyone can see,
Makes Tommy angry as can be.

—Eliot Kays Stone

A Message

I am sure that Spring is here,
   I'll tell you how I know;
The gayest little robin
   Sweetly told me so.

He stood upon my window sill
   And sang his song to me:
"Spring is here," he said to me,
   As plainly as could be.

          —Maud M. Goetting

Valentine

I made a snow man yesterday
   So jolly, fat, and fine,
I pinned a red heart on his chest
   And named him "Valentine."

Last night a warm, sweet breeze blew by,
   And stole his heart so gay;
My snow man melted on the spot
   And quickly ran away!

          —Frances Gorman Risser

Stars

The stars are tiny daisies high,—
Opening and shutting in the sky,
And daisies are the stars below,—
Twinkling and sparkling as they grow.

—Unknown

Lazy Time

In summer, when the sun is high
And skies are very blue,
I love to lie flat on my back
With not a thing to do.

The tall, green trees reach up so far,
They almost touch the sky;
And like a fleet of clean, white ships,
The clouds go sailing by.

If I were only high enough,
I'd pick my cloud today,
And steer for far-off lands to see
How other children play.

But if I lie there very long,
Sometimes there seems to be
Just nothing in this whole wide world
But sky, green trees, and me.

—Jean Gray Allen

My Airedale Dog

I have a funny Airedale dog,
  He's just about my size,
With such a serious-looking face,
  And eyes that seem so wise.

And he is just as full of tricks
  As any dog could be,
And we have mighty jolly times
  Because he plays with me,

And never tries to bite or snap;
  He doesn't even whine,—
And that is why my Airedale dog
  Is such a friend of mine.

          —W. L. Mason

Brooms

On stormy days
  When the wind is high
Tall trees are brooms
  Sweeping the sky.

They swish their branches
  In buckets of rain,
And swash and sweep it
  Blue again.

          —Dorothy Aldis

How They Sleep

Some things go to sleep in such a funny way:
Little birds
Stand on one leg and tuck their heads away;

Chickens do the same, standing on their perch;
Little mice
Lie soft and still as if they were in church;

Kittens curl up close in such a funny ball;
Horses hang
Their sleepy heads and stand still in a stall;

Sometimes dogs stretch out, or curl up in a heap;
Cows lie down
Upon their sides when they would go to sleep.

But little babies dear are snugly tucked in beds,
Warm with blankets,
All so soft, and pillows for their heads.

Bird and beast and babe—I wonder which of all
Dream the dearest dreams
That down from dreamland fall!

—Unknown

Group 13. <u>s</u> and <u>z</u>—continued*

Days

Some days my thoughts are just cocoons—
   all cold, and dull, and blind,
They hang from dripping branches
   in the gray woods of my mind;

And other days they drift and shine—
   such free and flying things!
I find the gold-dust in my hair,
   left by their brushing wings.

—Karle Wilson Baker

Starry Nights

New Moon

A single slender sickle reaps
   The fields of endless shade;
A host of flickering stars now leaps
   From the edge of the swinging blade.

Half Moon

The golden bowl, tipped at the rim,
   Has spilled into the dark
These countless jewels, each a gem
   Lit by a central spark.

Full Moon

Behold the form of a silver spider
   Crawling across the skies,
Spinning his web ever wider and wider,
   Snaring the bright fireflies.

—Leonard Twynham

---

* NOTE: For additional poems for "s" and "z," see pages 206 and 207.

Group 14. <u>sh</u>

Curly Locks

Curly Locks, Curly Locks,
  Wilt thou be mine?
Thou shalt not wash dishes
  Nor yet feed the swine,
But sit on a cushion
  And sew a fine seam
And feed upon strawberries,
  Sugar and cream.

—Mother Goose

When I Go Fishing

When I go fishing
I'm always wishing
Some fishes I will get;
But while I'm fishing,
The fish are wishing
I won't; just harder yet.

And all those wishes,
Of the fishes,
Every one come true;
So all my wishes
To get fishes
Never, never do.

—Unknown

Group 14. sh—continued

September

September is a lady
In a russet gown;
She marches through the country,
She marches through the town;
She stops at every schoolhouse
And rings a magic bell;
She dances on each doorstep
And weaves a magic spell.

She weaves a magic spell that goes
Winging through the land
And gathers children back to school
In a joyous band.

—Solveig Paulson

Ladybug

I wonder what the ladybug
Who lives by the wall
Does when it gets frosty
And cold in the fall;

She doesn't have a little fire,
She doesn't have a bed,
She doesn't have a jacket
Or a bonnet for her head,

She doesn't have a blanket,
Unless, do you suppose,
She finds herself a thistle down,
And covers up her nose?

—Aileen Fisher

Group 14. <u>sh</u>—continued*

The Moon

Does the moon know her name?
She must, seems to me,
'Cause otherwise how
Would she know she was she?

She may have found out
From the stars, or an elf,
But she MUST know, or how
Could she think of herself?

And besides, she must know
What her name is because
How else would she ever
Be sure who she was?

—Aileen Fisher

Nature's Wash Day

Mother Nature had a wash day
  And called upon the showers
To bathe the dusty faces
  Of the little roadside flowers.
She scrubbed the green grass carpet
  Until it shone like new.
She washed the faded dresses
  Of the oaks and maples, too.
No shady nook or corner
  Escaped her searching eye,
And then she sent the friendly sun
  To shine and make them dry.

—Marguerite Gode

---

* NOTE: For additional poems for "sh," see page 207.

The Chee-choo Bird

A little green bird sat on a fence rail
  Chee-choo, chee-choo, chee!
Its song was the sweetest I ever have heard
  Chee-choo, chee-choo, chee!
I ran for some salt to put on its tail
  Chee-choo, chee-choo, chee!
But while I was gone, away flew the bird
  Chee-choo, chee-choo, chee!

          —Unknown

The 'Chewy' Child

I know a funny little child.
  He chews up everything.
He chews up bits of paper,
  And he chews up balls of string.
He chews big chunks of chewing gum.
  All day I watch him chew.
I'm not surprised that when he talks
  He chews his words up, too.

          —L. D. S.

Little Charlie Chipmunk

Little Charlie Chipmunk was a talker. Mercy me!
He chattered after breakfast and he chattered after tea!
He chattered to his father and he chattered to his mother!
He chattered to his sister and he chattered to his brother!
He chattered till his family was almost driven wild
Oh, little Charlie Chipmunk was a very tiresome child!

—Helen Cowles LeCron

Desserts

Mother likes chestnuts,
Round roasted chestnuts.

Nancy likes chocolates,
Father likes a peach.

Beth likes a doughnut,
Cherries and cocoanut.

Jerry likes jelly rolls
    I
    like
    some
    of
    each!

—Aileen Fisher

The Little Toy Land of the Dutch

Away, way off 'cross the seas and such
Lies the little flat land of the Dutch, Dutch, Dutch!

Where the green toy meadows stretch off to the sea,
With a little canal where a fence ought to be!

Where the windmills' arms go round, round, round,
And sing to the crows with a creaky sound.

Where storks live up in the chimney top,
And wooden shoes pound, plop, plop, plop!

Where little toy houses stretch in a row,
And dog carts chattering past them go!

Where milk cans shine in the shiniest way,
And the housemaids scrub, scrub, scrub all day.

Where dikes keep out the raging sea,
And shut in the land as cozy as can be.

Oh, that little toy land, I like it much,
That prim little, trim little, land of the Dutch.

—Unknown

---

* NOTE: For additional poems for "ch," see page 207.

Jack, Be Nimble

Jack, be nimble,
　Jack, be quick;
Jack, jump over
　The candlestick!
　　　　　—Mother Goose

Blackbirds

There were two blackbirds
　Sitting on a hill,
One named Jack
　And the other named Jill.
Fly away, Jack!
　Fly away, Jill!
Come back, Jack!
　Come back, Jill!
　　　　　—Mother Goose

Mr. Jumping Jack

Mr. Jumping Jack is a very funny man,
He jumps and jumps as fast as he can.
His arms fly out, his feet fly too.
"Mr. Jumping Jack, How do you do?"
　　　　　—Unknown

Thanksgiving

As little Jackie Squirrel
    Looked out one Autumn day,
He saw old Mrs. Turkey,
    Who chanced to pass that way.

"She looks quite fine," said Jackie,
    "But I believe somehow;
I'd rather be a squirrel
    Than any bird just now!"

—Mrs. Cecil Trout Blancké

Joy

Joy is like a magic cup
    I lift it to the sky,
And all the more I offer up,
    The fuller joy have I.

—Unknown

---

* NOTE: For additional poems for "j," see page 207.

Group 17. y

Daffodil

A little yellow cup
A little yellow frill,
A little yellow star
And that's a daffodil.

—Unknown

Can You?

Can you hop like a rabbit?
Can you jump like a frog?
Can you walk like a duck?
Can you run like a dog?

Can you fly like a bird?
Can you swim like a fish?
And be still, like a good child
As still as you wish?

—Mildred Evans

Miss Daffodil

"Where did you, Miss Daffodil,
Get your pretty dress?
Is it made of golden sunshine?"
"Yes, child, yes."

—Anonymous

Group 17. y—continued*

New Year

A year to be glad in,
And not to be sad in,
To gain in, to give in,
A happy new year.

A new year for trying
And never for sighing;
A new year to live in;
Oh, hold it most dear!

—Unknown

The Dandelion

"O dandelion, yellow as gold,
What do you do all day?"
"I just wait here in the tall green grass
Till the children come to play."

"O dandelion, yellow as gold,
What do you do all night?"
"I wait and wait till the cool dew falls
And my hair grows long and white."

"And what do you do when your hair is white,
And the children come to play?"
"They take me up in their dimpled hands,
And blow my hair away."

—Unknown

---

* NOTE: For additional poems for "y," see page 207.

Cookies

Kate made some cookies
   For Kitty and me
And then put the cooky jar
   High as could be!
The stool tumbled over—
   Why couldn't Kate see
'Twas certain to happen
   To Kitty and me?

        —J. B. T.

Biddy Hen and Yellow Duck

Biddy Hen said
   "Cluck! Cluck! Cluck!
I do not like you,
   Yellow Duck!"

        —Unknown

Kittens·

A kitten with a black nose
   Will sleep all the day;
A kitten with a white nose
   Is always glad to play;
A kitten with a yellow nose
   Will come when you call;
But a kitten with a gray nose
   I like best of all.

        —Unknown

The Crocus

The golden crocus reaches up
To catch a sunbeam in her cup.

—Walter Crane

Drawing

I can paint pictures,
I can make letters,
I can draw figures of ladies and men.
I can draw kittens,
And mufflers, and mittens,
And Frenchmen, and Britons,
And even a hen!
I can make sketches
Of wide open stretches,
I can draw fishes—a trout and a pike,
I can paint witches,
And trousers and breeches,
And broomsticks and switches . . .

BUT

They all look alike!

—Aileen Fisher

* NOTE: For additional poems for "k," see page 207.

To Market, To Market

To market, to market, to buy a fat pig,
Home again, home again, jiggety-jig;
To market, to market, to buy a fat hog,
Home again, home again, jiggety-jog;
To market, to market, to buy a plum bun,
Home again, home again, market is done.

—Mother Goose

Where Are You Going, My Little Cat?

Where are you going, my little cat?
I am going to town to get me a hat.
What! a hat for a cat!
A cat get a hat!
Who ever yet saw a cat with a hat?

Where are you going, my little kittens?
We are going to town to get us some mittens.
What! Mittens for kittens!
Do kittens want mittens?
Who ever yet saw little kittens with mittens?

Where are you going, my little pig?
I am going to town to get me a wig.
What! A wig for a pig!
A pig in a wig!
Who ever yet saw a pig with a wig?

—Eliza Lee Follen

Little Girl, Little Girl

"Little girl, little girl, where have you been?"
"Gathering roses to give to the Queen."
"Little girl, little girl, what gave she you?"
"She gave me a diamond as big as my shoe."

—Mother Goose

Gold

My uncle was a miner
   And he found a lot of gold.
I used to like to listen
   To the stories that he told.

I'll never be a miner,
   But I found a pot of gold
Just going through the garden—
   'Twas a clump of marigold.

—J. B. T.

Not What We Give

Not what we give, but what we share,
For the gift without the giver is bare;
Who gives himself with his alms feeds three,
Himself, his hungering neighbor, and me.

—James Russell Lowell

---

* NOTE: For additional poems for "g," see page 207.

March

The wind is blowing 'round the house
  It's blowing, blowing, blowing.
The big trees shake and bow and bend.
  It's snowing, snowing, snowing.
But on the bushes little buds
  Are growing, growing, growing.
I saw a robin. Winter time
  Is going, going, going.

—Mildred Evans

Swinging

When I am swinging in my swing,—
I always have a song to sing;
A song about the lonely sky,
And of the swallows flying high.

One day when I was swinging fast,
I heard the bees go bumbling past;
They hummed a funny little tune,
About the flower-buds in June.

Sometimes I hardly see my toes,—
It's just the way the swinging goes.
It is such fun to have a swing,—
Don't you see why I have to sing?

—Marion E. Thorpe Diller

---

* NOTE: For additional poems for "ng," see page 207.

Group 21. h

My Hobby Horse

I had a little hobby horse,
　His name was Tommy Gray,
His head was made of peas straw,
　His body made of hay;
I saddled him and bridled him,
　And rode him up to town,
There came a little puff of wind
　And blew him up and down.

—Nursery Rhyme

The Blacksmith

The blacksmith hammers the whole day long,
His hammer is heavy, but his arm is strong.
Here comes a horse—what will blacksmith do?
He will hammer out a strong iron shoe.

—Old English Song

Santa Claus

A jolly old fellow,
Whose hair is snow white,
And whose little, bright eyes are blue,
Will be making his visits
On Christmas night;
Perhaps he will call on you.

—Unknown

The Crocus

The crocus had slept in his little round house
    So soundly the whole winter through;
There came a tap-tapping,—'twas Spring at the door:
    "Up! up! we are waiting for you."

The crocus peeped out from his little brown house
    And nodded his gay little head:
"Good morning, Miss Snowdrop, and how do you do
    This fine, chilly morning?" he said.

          —Sarah J. Day

Cock-a-Doodle-Doo

My neighbor has a herd, my neighbor has a flock,
But I have a barn with a gilt weathercock.
I have no horses, I have no hay,
But I have a weathercock, gilt and gay.
My neighbor has a flock, my neighbor has a herd,
But I have a beautiful bright tin bird.

And when I am dead, this will be said:
He had a weathercock on his shed,
He had no herd, he had no flock,
But he had a barn with a gilt weathercock;
He had no horses, he had no hay,
But he had a weathercock, gilt and gay;
His neighbor had a flock, his neighbor had a herd,
But he had a beautiful bright tin bird.

          —Richard Kirk

---

* NOTE: For additional poems for "h," see page 207.

INDEXES

INDEX OF POEMS ACCORDING TO SOUNDS*

* Since many of the poems provide practice for more than one sound, this cross-reference index is provided for the convenience of the teacher.

INDEX OF POEMS ACCORDING TO SOUNDS—continued

INDEX OF POEMS ACCORDING TO SOUNDS—continued

INDEX OF TITLES

INDEX OF TITLES—continued

INDEX OF TITLES—continued

INDEX OF TITLES—continued

INDEX OF FIRST LINES OF POEMS

INDEX OF FIRST LINES OF POEMS—continued

ALPHABETICAL INDEX FOR WORD DRILLS

* Includes both word drill and sentences.

* Includes both word drills and sentences.